T0334032

Special Economic Zones in India

This book systematically evaluates the trajectories of SEZs policymaking in India and its performance. The findings of the study are the result of a detailed fieldwork conducted by the author in India and China at different points in time. Exploring China's SEZs policy and performance the book discusses whether the Indian policymakers were aware of the nuances of the China's SEZs policy and the various facets of performance before replicating it for India. Performance analyses of Indian SEZs are carried out using both conventional set of performance indicators and new framework such as zone trade performance index, resource cost framework and efficiency analysis. The book offers a balanced view to rate the performance of Indian SEZs. In absolute terms, though performance of Indian SEZs scores better, this becomes questionable on the ground of fiscal viability of SEZs projects and efficiency in the production process. Variations in performance across zones explored with the help of zone trade performance index highlight the need to attend zone and sector specific problems and prospects. The significance of this study lies in its quest for providing a holistic appraisal of the various unexplored issues in the literature pertaining to SEZs in India. Through providing methodological contributions, the book suggests a new set of framework to analyse the performance of SEZs and appropriate policy directives for shaping SEZs as engines of growth.

Malini L. Tantri is Assistant Professor at the Centre for Economic Studies and Policy, Institute for Social and Economic Change (ISEC), Bangalore, India. Her areas of specialization include international trade and development – trade facilitation, India China studies, trade and gender, special economic zones and food security. Dr Tantri had previously worked at the Indian Institute of Technology Ropar, and also had assignments to assist the Government of Lao PDR to review the Draft of Prime Minister's Decree on SEZs.

Special Economic Zones in India
Policy, Performance and Prospects

Malini L. Tantri

CAMBRIDGE
UNIVERSITY PRESS

CAMBRIDGE
UNIVERSITY PRESS

4843/24, 2nd Floor, Ansari Road, Daryaganj, Delhi - 110002, India

Cambridge University Press is part of the University of Cambridge.

It furthers the University's mission by disseminating knowledge in the pursuit of education, learning and research at the highest international levels of excellence.

www.cambridge.org
Information on this title: www.cambridge.org/9781107109544

© Malini L. Tantri 2016

First published 2016

Printed in India by Shree Maitrey Printech Pvt. Ltd., Noida

A catalogue record for this publication is available from the British Library

Library of Congress Cataloging-in-Publication Data

Names: Tantri, Malini L., author.
Title: Special economic zones in India: policy, performance and prospects / Malini Tantri.
Description: New York : Cambridge University Press, 2016. | Includes bibliographical references and index.
Identifiers: LCCN 2016002556 | ISBN 9781107109544 (hardback)
Subjects: LCSH: Economic zoning--India.
Classification: LCC HC435.3 .T353 2016 | DDC 338.954--dc23 LC record available at http://lccn.loc.gov/2016002556

ISBN 978-1-107-10954-4 Hardback

Contents

List of Tables, Figures, Charts and Maps

Tables

Annexure tables

Figures

Charts

Maps

Preface

The study has been conceived, designed and carried out in the context of debates and discussions over the introduction of special economic zone (SEZ) policy in the country. The SEZ policy in India, based on the experience of China's SEZs, has been operating in the place of conventional export processing zones (EPZs) in pursuance of the recommendations of the EXIM Policy Statement of 1997–2002. This, in the present context, is considered a powerful instrument for export promotion and therefore, an alternative development strategy. Currently, SEZs have witnessed more than a decade in terms of their expansion in the country while receiving both appreciation and apprehension from different quarters. In this context it is quite necessary to find out whether China's SEZs are as promising as claimed by Indian policymakers or whether there are any issues overlooked while imitating China's model in the Indian context; whether the current SEZ policy merely represents old wine in a new bottle or whether there any new functionalities; how far the existing SEZs have been able to meet the expectations of policymakers; whether there are any basic loopholes still persisting in the current SEZ policy and the way forward. Against this background, this book attempts to evaluate the trajectories of the SEZ policy and its performance in India. Therefore, the main objectives of the study are as follows: first, to look at the Chinese SEZ policy and its varied experience from India's perspective; in particular, to probe whether the Indian policymakers were aware of the nuances of the China's SEZs policy and the various facets of its performance before replicating the same in the Indian context; and second, to understand the different dimensions of the policy and its performance.

The book spreads over seven chapters, starting with an 'Introduction'. Chapter 2 presents a discussion on the trajectories of the SEZ policy in India. The underpinnings of China's SEZ policy and its growth trajectories are discussed in chapter 3. The issue to what extent the existing SEZs have been able to meet the expectations of the policymakers, both at the aggregate and disaggregate levels, has been explored in chapter 4. While questioning the conventional parameters of performance, chapters 5 and 6 provide alternative techniques for evaluating the performance of SEZs. In particular, chapter 5 deals with the issue of fiscal implications of SEZs expansion in India. The issue of efficiency of SEZs as part of the trade policy as well as factors contributing to it, is discussed in chapter 6. Chapter 7 sums up the major findings along with empirical evidence based suggestions for policy revision.

Acknowledgements

A journey of a thousand miles begins with a small step … There are a lot of people who directly and indirectly encouraged me, boosted my confidence and helped me to initiate and finish this book. I take this opportunity to thank them sincerely and express my gratitude to them. Since this book is an outcome of my PhD thesis, my first and foremost debt undoubtedly is to my PhD supervisor, Professor R. S. Deshpande. He not only takes credit of helping me to understand the nuances of research but also extended unconditional and consistent support always. In this context, I also acknowledge University of Mysore, for giving me permission to publish my PhD thesis. I also acknowledge the timely interventions of Professor M. V. Nadakarni, Professor Michel Walton, Professor Alakh N. Sharma, Professor D. Narayana, Professor Chaya Degaonkar, Dr C. Veeramani and Dr M. VijayaBhaskar.

It would have been impossible to undertake study on special economic zone without the support and encouragement of the Ministry of Commerce and Industry, GoI. Special thanks are due to Mr Jayant Dasgupta, Ms Vandana Aggarwal, Mr Yoginder Garg, Mrs B. Ravindran and Ms Malini Shankar. I also acknowledge the cooperation and support of the Development Commissioner Officers and office bearers of Kandla, Santacruz, Noida, Cochin, Chennai, Falta and Vizag SEZs and also Export Promotion Council for SEZs and Export-oriented Units and Zone-level exporting units association. I also take this opportunity to register my sincere thanks to the Indian Council of Social Science Research (ICSSR) for providing financial assistance to undertake fieldwork in Beijing and Shenzhen in China, under the scheme of 'Data Collection Abroad' (2007) and also granting me a fellowship under 'India – China Economic and Cultural Exchange Programme to visit China' (2013). I also express my sincere thanks to senior academicians, officials of different organization, institutes and government agencies of Beijing, Shenzhen, Shanghai and Chengdu for their valuable inputs, information and cooperation during my fieldwork in China.

I also take this opportunity to submit my sincere gratitude to all the journal editorial teams and publishers for giving me permission to reproduce the articles in this present book form. For instance, fifth chapter of this book was originally published as: 'Fiscal Implications of Special Economic Zones (SEZs) in India: A Resource Cost Approach', Malini L. Tantri, *Journal of International Commerce, Economics and Policy*, Vol. 6, Issue No. 1, Copyright@ 2015, World Scientific Publishing Co. Pte. Ltd. Accordingly, due acknowledgment has been given wherever it is applicable.

Without the continuous encouragement, inspiration and blessings of my parents, other family members and friends like Varadu, Ranu and Soumya I would not have been able to undertake research. Especially my husband, Nalin, and my little daughter, Sandra have been very supportive throughout last few months of hectic work. I highly owe them for whatever I am today.

Abbreviations

AE	Allocative Efficiency
ANOVA	Analysis of Variance
AP	Andhra Pradesh
APO	Asian Productive Organization
APR	Annual Performance Report
BCA	Benefit Costs Analysis
BGMEA	Bangladesh Garments Manufacturer Exporters Association
BoA	Board of Approval
BoPs	Balance of Payments
CAGR	Compound Annual Growth Rate
CAGR	Compound Annual Growth Rate
CASS	Chinese Academy of Social Science
CBDT	Central Board of Direct Taxes
CBEC	Central Board of Excise and Customs
CG	Capital Goods
CRR	Cash Reserve Ratio
CSEZ	Cochin Special Economic Zone
CST	Central Sales Tax
CSY	China Statistical Year Book
DC	Development Commissioner
DDT	Dividend Distribution Tax
DEA	Data Envelopment Technique
DRC	Domestic Resource Cost
DTA	Domestic Trade Zone
EHTP	Electronic Hardware Technology Park
EOI	Export Oriented Industrialization

EOUs	Export Oriented Units
EP	Exports Promotion
EPC	Export Promotion Council
EPZ	Export Processing Zone
ETDZ	Economic and Technological Development Zones
EXIM	Export Import Policy
FDI	Foreign Direct Investment
FERA	Foreign Exchange Regulation Act
FIAS	Foreign Investment Advisory Service
FSEZ	Falta Special Economic Zone
FTP	Foreign Trade Policy
FTZ	Free Trade Zone
G & J	Gems and Jewellery
GDP	Gross Domestic Product
GoI	Government of India
GP	General Profile
GVOI	Gross Value Output of Industrial Sector
HDI	Human Development Index
HRS	Household Registration System
ICEC	India China Economic and Cultural Change
ICRIER	Indian Council for Research on International Economic Relation
II	Import Intensity
IID	Independently and Identically Distributed
IIE	Import Intensity of Exports
IIFT	Indian Institute of Foreign Trade
ILO	International Labour Organization
IMF	International Monetary Fund
ISI	Import Substitution Industrialization
IT	Information Technology
ITC	International Trade Centre

J&K	Jammu and Kashmir
KM	Kilometre
KAFTZ	Kandla Free Trade Zone
KSEZ	Kandla Special Economic Zone
MAT	Minimum Alternative Tax
MoCI	Ministry of Commerce and Industry
MRTP	Monopolies and Restrictive Trade Practices
MSEZ	Madras/Chennai Special Economic Zone
NDA	National Democratic Alliance
NEP	New Economic Policy
NFE	Net Foreign Exchange
NRI	Non-Resident Indian
NSEZ	Noida Special economic Zone
NTB	Non-Tariff Barriers
NTM	Non-Tariff Measures
OBU	Off Shore Banking Units
OECD	Organisation for Economic Co-operation and Development
OGL	Open General License
OLS	Ordinary Least Square
PCI	Per Capita Income
PRC	People Republic of China
R&D	Research and Development
R&R	Rehabilitation and Resettlement
RBI	Reserve Bank of India
RC	Resource Costs
RM	Raw Material
Rs	Rupees
SAP	Structural Adjustment Programme
SCM	Subsidies and Countervailing Measures
SDF	Standard Design Factory

SEZ Rule	Special Economic Zone Rule
SEZ	Special Economic Zone
SEZs Act	Special Economic Zone Act
SOE	State Owned Enterprises
SSEPZ	Santacruz Export Processing Zone
SSEZ	Santacruz Special Economic Zone
SSI	Small-Scale Industries
STPI	Software Technology Park of India
SZSEZ	Shenzhen Special Economic Zone
SZSY	Shenzhen Statistical Year Book
TDA	Trade Development Authority
TE	Technical Efficiency
TP	Trade Performance
TPI	Trade Performance Index
UAE	United Arab Emirates
UNCTAD	United Nation Conference on Trade and Development
UNCTC	United Nation Centre on Transitional Corporation
UNDP	United Nations Development Programme
UNIDO	United Nation Industrial Development Organization
UPA	United Progressive Alliance
USA	Unites States of America
USAID	United State Agency for Industrial Development
USSR	Union of Soviet Socialistic Republic
VAT	Value Added Tax
VSEZ	Vizag Special Economic Zone
WB	World Bank
WEPZA	World Exports Processing Zones Association Zones
WTO	World Trade Organization
Z-TPI	Zone-Trade Performance Index

1

Introduction

Background

Special economic zones (SEZs) have a long economic pedigree in the context of India as well as other countries. From a global perspective, in today's context, SEZs are a modified version of the conventional export processing zones (EPZs), which again are a combination of two older instruments, viz., industrial estate/industrial park and free zone/free trade zone (FTZ) (World Bank, 1992). 'Industrial estate' refers to a geographical area allotted for industrial development. This concept emerged in the industrialized countries towards the end of the nineteenth century.[1] However, FTZs were set up near airports or seaports areas, which were free from customs duties. These facilities were used for storing transaction goods. The fusion of two ideas, that is, industrial estate and FTZ, provided a basic framework for the emergence of EPZs, which were customized for the promotion of non-traditional exports. The world's first and full-fledged EPZ came up in Ireland in 1959 (World Bank, 1992), and thereafter, within a short span of time, the concept of EPZs spread all over the world, particularly the developing economies. India and Puerto Rico were at the forefront in popularizing EPZs as an instrument of trade. In India, the first attempt in this direction was made in 1964, as part of an inward looking trade strategy, followed by other developing countries such as Taiwan, Philippines, the Dominican Republic, Mexico, Panama and Brazil during the period between 1966–70 (Wong and Chu, 1985).

It is undeniable that neither India nor China invented or pioneered the SEZ concept; rather, it is fair to believe that it evolved over the centuries

---

1   The world's first full-fledged industrial estate was set up in 1896 as a private commercial venture at Trafford Park in Manchester, England (World Bank, 1992).

through permutations and combinations of different practices prevailing in many parts of the world. In fact, the number of EPZs increased sharply from 79 (spread over 25 countries) in 1975 to 6,000 (spread over 130 countries) by the end of 2006. The initial stimulus and growth of these zones could be attributed to the failure of the inward looking trade strategy that was in vogue in most of these economies. This was true particularly in the case of developing countries throughout Asia. The success of EPZs in later years was due to demonstration effect of the successful experience of the earlier zones, i.e., those established in the 1960s and 1970s.

Further, a look at the spread of EPZs across major geographical zones of the world reveals that Central American countries and Mexican, followed by Asian countries, were at the forefront in the promotion of EPZs (Table 1.1). The Asian zones, however, hold the record for having generated more employment opportunities as compared to the Central and Latin American countries. This could be due to the sectoral composition and type of investment attracted by these zones and the comparative advantage they enjoy in respect of producing labour-intensive products in the Asian region. However, different terminologies are being used across countries to define the concept of SEZs (Table 1.2). Diversity in its terminology reflects its evolutionary nature and the distinct purposes behind the establishment of zones across countries (Armas and Sadni-Lallab, 2002). These zones can be categorized into manufacturing, trading and service zones. Further, the terms used also speak of the physical characteristics of zones, type of activities involved, incentives and permission given for domestic or overseas sales, etc.

Table 1.1: Size and Employment in EPZs/SEZs across the World

Geographical regions	Number of zones	Employment (million)
Asia • of which China • of which BGMEA* factories in Bangladesh	749	37 (30) (0.20)
Central America and Mexico	3300	0.22
Middle East	37	0.7
North Africa	23	0.4
Sub-Saharan Africa	64	0.4
North America	713	0.3

Geographical regions	Number of zones	Employment (million)
South America	39	0.3
Transition economies	90	0.2
Caribbean	87	0.22
Indian Ocean	3	0.1
Europe	55	0.051
Pacific	14	0.014
Total	**5,174**	**42**

Note: *BGMEA refers Bangladesh Garments Manufacturer Exporters Association.
Source: ILO (2006).

Table 1.2: Different Terminologies used for EPZs/SEZs

Synonyms	Studies, countries and date of first use
Free Trade Zone	Traditional term since the nineteenth century
Foreign Trade Zone	Individual authors (R. S. Toman, 1956; W. Dymsza, 1964), India (1983)
Industrial Free Zone	Ireland (pre–1970), UNIDO (1971), Liberia (1975)
Free Zone	UNCTAD (1973), USAID (1982), United Arab Emirates (1983)
Maquiladoras (in-bond) Enterprises	Mexico (early 1970s), Costa Rica, Honduras, Ireland, Trinidad and Tobago, Turkey, United Arab Emirates, Uruguay, Venezuela
Export Free Zone	Ireland (1975), UNIDO (1976)
Duty Free Export Processing Zone	Republic of Korea (1975)
Export Processing Free Zone	UNIDO (1976), UNCTAD (1983)
Free Production Zone	Sternberg Institute (1977)
Export Processing Zone	Philippines (1977), Harvard University (1977), APO (1977), WEPZA (1978), UNIDO (1979), Malaysia (1980), Pakistan (1980), Singapore (1982), UNCTC (1982), ILO (1983)

Synonyms	Studies, countries and date of first use
Tax Free Trade Zone	Individual author (D. B. Diamond, 1980)
Investment Promotion Zone	Sri Lanka (1981)
Free Economic Zone	Individual author (H. Grubel, 1982)
Free Export Zone	Republic of Korea (1983)
Free Export Processing Zone	OECD (1984)
Special Economic Zone	China (1979), India (2000)
Industrial Estates	Thailand
'Points francs' (Special Industrial Free Zones)	Cameroon
Bonded Zone	Indonesia
Tax Free Factories	Fiji
Industrial Free Zones for Goods and Services	Colombia

Source: Armas and Sadni - Lallab (2002), Kusago, and Tzannatos (1998), Government of India (1997).

In India, SEZs concept *per se* was introduced in the EXIM policy statement of 1997–2002, almost a decade after the introduction of India's reform process, and in response to challenges emerging out of the economic liberalization initiated the world over. In fact, SEZs represent a typical case of reform strategy with a number of adjustments made to the existing policy instrument along with a set of new instruments.[2] Nevertheless, India had done the required groundwork through the creation of FTZs/EPZs at Kandla in the early 1960s, as part of the government's efforts to have an alternative port set up in the western coast of India. This was later followed by the establishment of other zones in different parts of the country with different objectives underlying their promotion. Thus, the present SEZ policy came to be is executed in two different stages in India. Initially, all the existing EPZs, that is, Kandla, Santacruz, Noida, Chennai, Cochin, Falta, Vizag and Surat were brought under the SEZs scheme. We refer to these as the conventional SEZs of the country. This was later followed by the approval of fresh SEZs

---

2 Details of major differences between the pre-reform and post-reform periods have been outlined in flow chart 1.1.

in the country, and these are referred to as new SEZs in this study.[3] Currently, SEZs have completed more than a decade since their introduction in the country and during this period they have received both bouquets and brickbats from different quarters on a wide range of issues pertaining to their establishment.

Chart 1.1: The Evolution of Trade Policy through the Pre-reform and Post-reform Periods

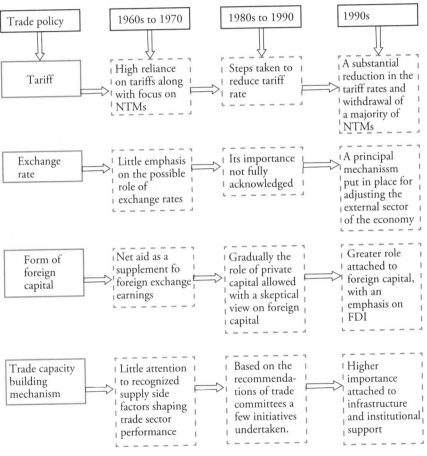

Source: Author.

Focus of the study

A survey of literature pertaining to India's SEZs (see for instance, Kundra, 2000; Aggarwal, 2004, 2005, 2007, 2010 and 2012; Mukhopadhay, 2007;

---

3   A detailed analysis of the SEZ policy has been carried out in Chapter 2.

Rao, 2007; Bhaduri, 2007; Sharma, 2007; Gill, 2007; Patnaik, 2007; Gopalakrishnan, 2007; Banerjee *et al.*, 2007; Palit and Bhattacharjee, 2007; Kasturi, 2008; Sampat, 2008; Shah, 2009; Mukhopodyay, 2009; Menon and Mitra, 2009; Laxmanan, 2009; Gupta, 2008 and 2009; Carter, 2010; Levien, 2011; Sundarapandian, 2012; Cook *et al.*, 2013), against the backdrop of such growing academic interests, reveals that most of these studies are kind of piecemeal effort and what is missing is a holistic appraisal of SEZs expansion in India. In fact, studies pertaining to India's EPZs/SEZs could be categorized into two broad groups. The first category covers studies that evaluated the performance of these enclaves based on different parameters. Within this, a few studies attempt time-series analyses, cross-country comparisons and contextual analyses specifically in terms of assessing the capacity of emerging SEZs in meeting different expectations of the policymakers. The second set of studies consists largely of debates over current SEZ policy of the country from land, resettlement, rehabilitation to environmental considerations. Undoubtedly, these studies fail to address a few pertinent issues such as before introducing SEZs in India based on China's experience whether we had a sufficient understanding of the factors that boosted their performance and whether China's SEZs were really as promising as hypothesized by Indian policymakers? Whether the current SEZ policy merely represents old wine in a new bottle or whether there are any new functionalities? Whether there exists any basic loopholes not addressed by the current SEZ policy? How far operational SEZs have been able to meet the expectations of policy makers? To what extent are the conventional indicators of performance parameters appropriate? If not, what are the other appropriate techniques for evaluating their performance? With this background in view, this book attempts to provide certain critical insights into various pertinent issues surrounding the expansion of SEZs in India. Specifically, the SEZ policy has been evaluated in terms of: (a) Exploring the very relevance of the idea underlying promotion of the present SEZs policy, i.e., did we have a clear idea of expected benefits and associated negative impacts of the intended policy; did we know the experience of a similar policy sufficiently well, if any, in respect of other countries – were they successful ventures or a flawed attempts and what factors would explain such outcomes? (b) Looking into the SEZ policy structure and its implementation process, does the SEZ policy represent old wine in a new bottle or whether there are any new functionalities and also whether there are any fundamental problems left unattended? (c) It evaluates the performance levels of SEZs in terms of both conventional indicators and a new set of frameworks.

Canvas of the study area and methodology

To explore whether there was logical clarity behind the promotion of SEZ policy, we have analysed the policy and performance experience of SEZs in China since India's SEZ policy has been modelled after China's SEZs. In particular, for an in-depth study, among the five full-fledged SEZs and 14 ETDZs of China, we have chosen Shenzhen SEZ for two reasons: (a) given its size, Shenzhen SEZ represents a classic case of an industrial township; and (b) its commanding performance according to the stated objectives relative to other SEZs and its transformation from a small fishing community into a full-fledged industrial township. The reference period of the study spans three decades from 1980 (post-SEZs) to 2012–13. The analysis is based on various policy documents related to China's SEZs, secondary data (*Chinese Statistical Year Book,* 2012 and *Shenzhen Statistical Year Book*, 2013) and the author's perception during an extended fieldwork in China.[4] However, it is to be noted that our aim here is not to draw any comparison between China's and India's SEZs; rather, the attempt is to understand China's SEZ policy and its experience from India's perspective, and to draw appropriate lessons so as to make India's SEZs more effective as a policy instrument.

Besides outlining China's SEZ policy and experience, the focus of the study is to analyse the dynamics underlying the promotion of SEZs in India and in particular, to trace the effectiveness of SEZ policy over EPZs of the country both in terms of policy document and performance. For this purpose, only those SEZs that were operating at least five years prior to the introduction of the SEZ policy (2000) in the country have been covered by this study, the reason being that new SEZs might not help locate the effectiveness of SEZs *vis-à-vis* EPZs. Accordingly, this study has covered seven conventional[5] SEZs operating across seven states. Thereby, it includes, Kandla SEZ (KSEZ) in

---

4 The fieldwork was carried out in 2007 (across two cities of China namely, Beijing and Shenzhen) and 2013 (across three cities of China namely, Beijing, Chengdu, Shanghai)

5 The currently operating SEZs in the country could be categorized under two major types – conventional SEZs and modern/new SEZs. Conventional SEZs are those which were operating under the EPZ structure of the country, currently brought under the SEZs scheme. Modern SEZs, however, are those which were approved after the enactment of the SEZs policy in the country.

Gujarat, Santacruz SEZ (SSEZ) in Maharashtra, Noida SEZ (NSEZ) of Uttar Pradesh, Chennai SEZ (MSEZ) in Tamil Nadu, Cochin SEZ (CSEZ) in Kerala, Falta SEZ (FSEZ) in West Bengal and Vizag SEZ (VSEZ) in Andhra Pradesh.[6] Excepting Santacruz, which has been promoted exclusively for the promotion of gems and jewellery and electronics industries, all other zones offer a multiproduct base to investors. An analysis of India's SEZ policy and performance is based on both secondary data published in various reports and documents and primary data collected through a survey. Information on policy changes and related information on India's SEZs has been gathered from SEZs Act 2005, SEZs Rule 2006, subsequent amendments, various reports and documents published by the Ministry of Commerce and Industry, respective state government gazettes, RBI annual reports on the Indian economy, economic survey of India, whereas the secondary data on India's SEZs from the respective Development Commissioner's office located in each zone, Ministry of Commerce and Industry, Export Promotion Council for SEZs and EOUs, and Export Promotion Council for Gems and Jewellery. Primary data[7] on India's SEZs was collected at two levels: at the first level, information was collected from officers in charge of different sections of Development Commissioner' office, Export Promotion Council for SEZs and EOUs, and zone associations; and at the second level, information was obtained from exporting units in each zone.

Table 1.3: SEZs Notified before the Enactment of SEZs Act, 2005 in India

Sl. No	Zone		Notified
Government SEZs (converted from EPZs)			
1	Kandla, Gujarat	SEZ (FTZ)	1964
2	Santacruz, Maharashtra	SEZ (EPZ)	1973–74
3	Noida, Uttar Pradesh	SEZ (EPZ)	1984–85
4	Chennai, Tamil Nadu	SEZ (EPZ)	1984–85
5	Cochin, Kerala	SEZ (EPZ)	1984–85
6	Falta, West Bengal	SEZ (EPZ)	1985–86
7	Vizag, Andhra Pradesh	SEZ (EPZ)	1986–87

6 Refer table 4.1 for brief description of seven SEZs covered by the study.
7 Primary data are based on fieldwork carried out between 2007 and 2014.

Sl. No	Zone	Notified
	SEZs Notified before Enactment of SEZs Act, 2005	
8	Surat, Gujarat SEZ	1 November 2002
9	Manikanchan, West Bengal SEZ	12 June 2003
10	Jaipur, Rajasthan SEZ	1 July 2003
11	Indore SEZ	1 August 2003
12	Jodhapur, Rajasthan SEZ	8 September 2003
13	Salt Lake Electronics city – WIPRO, West Bengal	12 August 2005
14	Mahindra City SEZ (IT), Tamil Nadu	26 October 2004
15	Mahindra City SEZ (auto ancillary), Tamil Nadu	
16	Mahindra City SEZ (textiles), Tamil Nadu	26 October 2004
17	Nokia, Tamil Nadu	7 December 2005
18	Moradabad SEZ	30 September 2003
19	Surat Apparel Park, Gujarat	31 January 2005

Source: www.sezindia.nic.in.

Organization of the book

The book is organized into seven chapters including of an introduction. The second chapter traces the evolution of India's SEZ policy. In particular, this chapter attempts a programmatic historical survey of EPZs/SEZs followed in India over the last five decades (1960 to till date), focusing especially on the possible reasons leading to the realization on the part of policymakers and the government that the existing EPZs required a radical overhauling both in terms of their objectives and the arms provided to bring this objectives to fruition, which in turn led to the transformation of EPZ into SEZs; to what extent has the transformation of EPZs into SEZs been effective at the construction and implementation levels; what are the problems and prospect of the current SEZ policy. Underpinnings of Chinese SEZ policy and its growth trajectories are outlined in chapter 3. In this chapter, in particular, we explore issues such as (a) factors contributing to the success of China's SEZ policy, as also various supportive mechanisms, both internal and external that have played an important role in scripting this success story; (b) inadequacies of India's policymakers in understanding the demands underlying such a policy shift and its implementation, and also the institutional and infrastructural requirements that should have been provided for its emulation; (c) the lessons that India can imbibe in its attempt to redefine the SEZ policy, which, doubtless, has become a necessity now.

How far have been the operational SEZs been able to meet the expectations of policymakers both at aggregate and disaggregate levels is an issue that has been discussed in the fourth chapter. While questioning the conventional parameters of performance, chapters 5 and 6 provide alternative techniques for evaluating the performance of SEZs. In particular, chapter 5 deals with the issue of fiscal implications of SEZs expansion in India. The issue of efficiency of SEZs as a trade policy as well as factors contributing to it are probed in the chapter 6. Chapter 7 summarizes the major findings along with suggestions for policy revision.

2

Export Processing Zones to Special Economic Zones: Trajectories of Policymaking

Background

SEZs have a long pre-history in the origins and evolution of EPZs, i.e., SEZs are basically the metamorphosis of EPZs, which existed in the Indian economy since 1960s. However, there is a very little in the literature that aims to provide a historical understanding of this evolution and metamorphosis. Explanation for such metamorphosis from EPZs to SEZs could be due to the following: (a) there might have been flaws in the idea behind promotion of EPZs and subsequently in articulating the EPZ policy; (b) there might have been failure in the execution of EPZ policy. These two possible reasons as speculated here are worthy of investigation. Furthermore, how so far the current SEZ policy meets the expectation of policymakers in these two criteria are worthy of exploration. With this background, this chapter attempts a programmatic historical survey of the EPZs/SEZs followed in India in the last five decades (from 1960 till date), focusing especially on the possible reasons that led to the realization on the part of policymakers and the government at large that the existing EPZs require a radical overhauling both in terms of their objectives and the arms that they have been provided in order to bring this objectives into fruition, which in turn led to the transformation of EPZs into SEZs; how far the transformation from EPZs to SEZs is effective at the construction and at the implementation level; what are the problems and prospectus of current SEZ policy. The exercise is based on analysis of various Acts, policy documents, trade reports, government ordinance and regulations and literature on this issue. The rest of the chapter is planned as follows. The next section outlines the evolution of SEZ policy in the country in the last five decades. The section on paradoxes of the current SEZ policy critically evaluates the major loopholes in the current SEZs period and outline prospects and paradoxes of the policy. The last section offers a brief summary.

Metamorphosis from EPZs to SEZ

There exists a close association between the approach followed for setting the economic priorities of the country and the policy evolved for shaping the structure of EPZs/SEZs. It is against this background that the evolution of the SEZ policy in the Indian context is explained here in two phases, stretching over the last five decades. The first phase guidelines emerged while framing the EPZs regime (from 1960s to 2000[1]). This could be regarded as the pre-SEZ regime because the earlier EPZs metamorphed into SEZs. This phase is further studied under two subphases: (a) the first subphase of EPZs expansion (1960–90) – the beginning of export promotion within import substitution industrialization (ISI) strategy; (b) economic reform and second subphase of EPZs expansion (1990–2000). The SEZ policy evolved by the Ministry of Commerce, Government of India, in the current context, specifically from 2000 onwards, could be regarded as the second phase.

First phase – expansion of the EPZs structure in India

First subphase of EPZs expansion (1960–90) – onset of export promotion within ISI strategy:

The evolution of the EPZ era in the country could be traced to a few export promotion measures introduced in the early 1960s on an experimental basis, specifically through setting up of the country's first free trade zone at Kandla (1965). The exercise to introduce the same, however, was initiated in the late 1950s with a view to promoting Kandla Port as a substitute for Karachi Port, which India lost at the time of partition[2] (Indian Institute of Foreign Trade, 1990). Initially, Kandla FTZ was assigned multiple objectives: (a) developing Kandla port as a substitute for Karachi port; (b) promoting 100 per cent export-oriented industries; and (c) promoting

---

1 It is to be noted that in the present exercise we have followed a completely different type of policy classification as compared to the previous studies (Kundra, 2000; Aggarwal, 2004, 2005) of the same.

2 Because Bombay Port had to face a severe work load, which was not the consistent with available infrastructure facilities.

industrial development in the region (ibid). Thus, trade promotion was not the sole purpose behind the promotion of an FTZ at Kandla. Nevertheless, the creation of the first FTZ at Kandla gave India the distinction of being a pioneer in experimenting with FTZs/EPZs in the Asian continent. Kandla was placed in one of the backward regions of Gujarat with a number of fiscal and non-fiscal incentives offered to attract investors (Table 2.1). Among others, it included the facilities such as availability of industrial units, an assurance of continuous supply of electricity and water at very reasonable prices[3] and also all the necessary infrastructure facilities. Subsequently, the Government of India established Santacruz EPZ (SEEPZ) in 1972, which became operational in 1973–74. Initially, it was promoted as a single-sector zone with an emphasis on electronic goods. However, in 1986, gems and jewellery were added to SEEPZ in view of a growing international market for this sector.

Table 2.1: Incentives Offered Initially (in the 1960s) to KFTZ

Sl. No.	Incentives
1	Exemption from central excise duty on finished products or a few raw materials as specified
2	Exemption from import duties on goods for the purpose of export
3	No need to obtain license as all imports for the zone purpose were listed under Open General License (OGL)
4	No excise duties on raw materials imported from the DTA
5	Facilities to access finance at concessional rates from Gujarat State Financial Corporation
6	Exemption from municipal tax
7	Exemption from octroi tax
8	Provision of cement, steel, telephone and telegraph facilities on priority basis
9	20 per cent of profit exempted from income tax for a period of 10 years
10	Reimbursement of central sales tax

Source: IIFT, 1990.

---

3   Water was provided at ₹ 0.40–0.65 per 1,000 litre depending on water consumption (IIFT, 1990).

Table 2.2: Incentives Offered Initially (in the 1970s) to SEEPZ

Sl. No.	Incentives
1	Import of capital goods, raw materials, components, tooling etc under OGL
2	Duty free import of capital goods and equipments
3	Exemption from customs and countervailing duties on all raw material, components, tooling, etc.
4	Exemption from central excise duties on products manufactured in the zone
5	Capital goods, raw materials, components, etc., supplied to the zone from the domestic tariff area were to be treated as exports and eligible for all concessions as applicable to exports from the country
6	A single point clearance of applications for industrial licensing capital goods imports, MRTP, FERA, etc., by a specifically constituted SEEPZ Board

Source: Review Committee on Electronics, 1979.

It should be noted here that, if one were to stick to nomenclature, Santacruz was the first EPZ of the country, and Kandla, the first and only FTZ in the country. Other than nomenclature, the major difference between the two lies in the history and prime objectives of their promotion. As stated above, the initial idea of creating an FTZ came soon after independence to make Kandla Port a substitute for Karachi port, which India lost at the time of partition (IIFT, 1990). SEEPZ, however, was proposed by Trade Development Authority (TDA) for the promotion of electronics industry after taking into consideration the growing international demand for electronic goods and services. A deeper look into the objectives behind the promotion of Kandla and Santacruz zones reveals divergent views of the decision makers with regard to the role and responsibilities assigned to these zones. Perhaps, among others, this could be considered as a factor responsible for the poor performance of EPZs. Later, this was emphasized by the Tandon Committee (1980) as well. This obviously came in conflict with policy initiatives needed for the promotion of these two different typologies of zones.

Till the late 70s, the performance of both the zones was dismal, leading to the rejection of demands from other states for setting up of analogous zones (Kundra, 2000). In the subsequent years, the Government of India appointed a few committees[4] to review the trade policy of the country in general and to evaluate the performance of these zones, in particular. These committees felt the need for reorienting the trade policy of the country towards export promotion. The Review Committee on Electronics (1979), while particularly commenting on the poor performance of SEEPZ, highlighted the following factors as being responsible for the poor performance: (a) facilities available to SEEPZ not being on par with the those offered by similar zones in the neighbouring countries; (b) long procedural formalities and the prevalence of red-tapism; and (c) inadequate powers given to the respective development commissioners. The committee also made a few recommendations for reshaping the working of SEEPZ. The major ones included:

- SEEPZ Board should be abolished and its duties and powers handed over to the development commissioner.

- Exemption from corporate tax and tax on dividends for SEEPZ units, existing and new ones, for five years with in-built provisions for reviewing the extension of 'tax holiday' on merit at the end of five years.

- A higher rate of depreciation for zonal units – at least 30 per cent a year.

- Abolition of service tax.

- Exemption from levies other than central customs/excise duties.

- Export credit/finance, market development grants for export promotion travels, sales, and publicity, etc., and the zonal units should be treated on par with exporting units in the hinterland.

Besides advocating a few incentives for exporting units, the committee also emphasized on those measures that might be helpful in reducing the cost of production and also improving the administrative structure of the country. Subsequently, the Tandon Committee (1980) felt that even after two decades of operation, there was no clarity with respect to the objectives for the promotion of such zones. At the same time, the committee also stressed the importance of such zones in the process of economic growth, specifically in terms of boosting exports of the country while recommending

---

4   It concludes: The Alexander Committee on Import and Export Policies (1978); the Review Committee on Electronics (1979); the Dagli Committee on Controls and Subsidies (1979); and the Committee on FTZs and 100 per cent EOUs (1982).

the creation of similar zones in other parts of the country. However, this recommendation was contrary to the one made by a committee (Cabinet Committee on Economic Policy and Co-ordination) constituted in the late 1970s, which had rejected the idea of setting up of similar zones in other parts of the country. The Tandon Committee (1980) also emphasized the need for providing high-quality infrastructure, institutions, and incentives to promote such zones. Accordingly, an inter-ministerial group set up in line with the recommendations of the Tandon Committee (1980), which proposed the establishment of EPZs at Salt Lake in West Bengal, Chennai in Tamil Nadu, Cochin in Kerala, Nava Sheva in Maharashtra, Vishakapattanam in Andhra Pradesh, Mudgaon Vasco in Goa and Noida in Uttar Pradesh (Kundra, 2000). However, EPZs were approved to be set up only at Cochin, Chennai, Falta and Noida[5] followed by the EPZ at Vishakapattanam.[6] Subsequently, the Abid Hussain Committee (1984) reiterated the policy failure to provide a conducive environment for meeting the expectations of these enclaves. The committee, therefore, recommended the following: (a) adoption of a single window clearance; (b) a selective approach towards selecting industries; and (c) the concession to sell 25 per cent of their output on the domestic market against valid import license to be continued.[7]

On the whole, this phase witnessed a very prudent approach towards the promotion of EPZs with a few EPZs coming into existence subsequently. Meanwhile, various committees were constituted periodically to suggest ways and means for improving the performance of trade sector in general and these zones in particular. However, the government lacked a consistent approach to rectify the supply side factors hindering the progress of EPZs. For instance, the government made efforts to identify a few more zones in the country as per the recommendation of the Tandon Committee (1980) but, at the same time, it overlooked the other recommendations with respect to improving the institutional and infrastructural facilities across the zones. Moreover, the issue of ownership, lethargic administration, cumbersome administrative procedures and other structural problems received very little attention on the policy front. As a result, all six EPZs were owned and managed by the central government, virtually becoming in the process,

---

5 They became functional in 1985–86.

6 It was approved in 1989 and became functional in 1994.

7 Refer Annexure Table 2.1, for major chronological policy developments during the different phases of SEZs expansion in India.

more like public sector units, with hardly any competition from other actors. The failure to provide better institutional arrangements for EPZs could be explained in terms of loopholes inherent in the pre-reform period economic policy of the country.

Economic reforms and the second sub-period (1990–2000)

The process of reshuffling the economic structure initiated in the 1990s (also known as the Structural Adjustment Programme) also had an impact on the working of EPZs through a good number of initiatives undertaken on the policy front. The major policy developments noticed in this period[8] included the extension of the working of these zones from traditional activities to agriculture (1992) and allowing the private sector to operate (1994). As part of the government commitment to promote private actors in such zones, the first private-based EPZ was set up in 1994 for the promotion of the gems and jewellery sector. This also symbolized a serious effort on the part of the government to rejuvenate EPZs by way of providing a larger area for their operation. Thus, such major steps towards creating a competitive environment for EPZs so as to enable them to compete in the world market took place in the post-reform period. This also signifies the lack of major policy directions in the first phase of the EPZ regime.

Despite these policy developments, the fundamental problems plaguing these EPZs remained unattended; specifically, there was no law governing the activities of EPZs in the country and it depended completely on the EXIM policy of the government. As a result, it was no surprise that issues such as cumbersome bureaucratic procedures, institutional- and infrastructure-related problems of these enclaves remained unattended. In fact, policymakers failed to identify the shortcomings of the Indian economy and to use the EPZs structure as a learning curve before spreading them across the nation.

Second phase: Emergence of the SEZs regime in India (2000 onwards)

The second phase of the evolution of the SEZ policy in India was based on the successful experience of SEZs in China with a reference made to it in the EXIM policy statement of 1997–2002. Accordingly, the SEZ policy was put in place in the country on 1 April 2000. A legal framework was instituted in 2005 through the enactment of SEZs Act, 2005, followed by SEZ Rules,

---

8   For further details, see Annexure Table 2.1 for detailed chronological developments in policy initiatives that took place in this first sub-period.

2006.[9] Besides, every state government enacted the state-specific SEZs acts and policies to push forward state-specific requirements through SEZs.

The current SEZ policy differs from the conventional EPZs structure on the following ground. Unlike the EPZ regime where only the public sector played an active role, the SEZ policy allows for entry of the private, public and/or joint sectors. Further, along with manufacturing activities, the service sector is also allowed to operate for trade purposes. Free trade and warehousing activities too have acquired a larger space for their operations. With regard to administration practice, the current SEZ policy has witnessed significant changes in respect of the management of SEZs as against the earlier practice, that is, greater powers are devolved from the apex level to the zonal level. Specifically, the Development Commissioner of each respective zone is made responsible not only for day-to-day operations but also to decide on the nature of enterprises to be allowed and labour-related issues. Besides, another striking feature of the current SEZ policy relates to the recognition of the role of academicians in the approval of SEZs though their role remains only nominal in that they do not make any effective intervention. Apart from facilitating decentralization in the administrative structure, the role of respective state governments is duly recognized in the SEZ structure. This provision, however, was missing in the EPZ scheme. The roles and responsibilities assigned to state governments under the current SEZ policy include forwarding proposals for the creation of SEZs to the Board of Approval (BoA). In this respect, the respective state governments are required to ensure that proposal forwarded for the establishment of SEZs are in accordance with the provisions specified in the SEZ rules of 2006, particularly with respect to the minimum area of land and other related terms and conditions. At the same time, they also need to indicate whether the proposed area falls under the reserved or ecologically fragile area as may be specified by the authority concerned; before recommending any proposal for setting up SEZs, the respective state government shall ensure that the required infrastructure facilities are provided and steps taken to adhere to various terms as enlisted in the SEZs Act (Government of India, 2005 and 2006).

Thus, a prior consent of the respective state governments regarding the feasibility of SEZs and whether they are in a position to provide the required infrastructure facilities are crucial to the whole process. The state

9   Following this, a few amendments have been effected to the SEZs Act and rules in the last few years.

governments concerned have also been given powers to introduce state-specific Acts, rules and regulations pertaining to SEZs, basically with respect to boosting investors' confidence and also highlight the state government's role in various aspects relating to state levies, generation and distribution of power, environmental clearance, etc. Keeping in line with the provisions, the respective state governments have taken policy decisions to address the state-specific development priorities. As a result, there exist variations across the states with respect to state-specific objectives (Table 2.3) and incentives offered to SEZs.[10] Further, very less is known as to whether objectives designed by the respective states fall in line with the comparative advantage of each state or whether they are designed arbitrarily. This provides scope for further research. Besides this, SEZ policy has taken the first step in terms of identifying and statutorily implementing a few provisions required to make doing business easily in a less expensive manner. For instance, the SEZ policy provides scope for single-window clearance for setting up units and all matters related to the central and state governments in addition to simplified procedures and documentations with an emphasis on self-certification – basically, any aspect related to customs. It also encourages setting up of Export Promotion Council (EPC) for SEZs and Export Oriented Units (EOUs). This acts largely as a platform for developers and unit-holders to express their concerns pertaining to doing business within SEZs and thereby at appropriate levels by EPC for SEZs and EOUs. It also acts as a channel for dissemination of the latest information pertaining to changes in the provisions of SEZ policy.

Table 2.3: Objectives Underlying SEZs across Major Indian States

Sl. No.	State	Objectives
1.	Karnataka	To attract foreign investment and augment exports from the state
2.	Orissa	To expand industrial and economic bases through optimum utilization of natural and mineral resources
3.	Tamil Nadu	To fetch substantial dividend to the state in terms of industrial and economic development and additional employment
4	Andhra Pradesh	To promote industrial development and enhanced job opportunities

---

10 The issue of incentives across major states is elaborated in the subsequent section.

Sl. No.	State	Objectives
5.	Rajasthan	To explore the inherent potential of the state in the fields of gems and jewellery, handicrafts, woollen carpets, etc. and to increase exports with high value addition
6.	Kerala	To create wealth and employment opportunities
7.	Maharashtra	To enhance productivity and ease of doing business in the state by providing simple and transparent administration procedures
8.	West Bengal	To effectively utilize the locally available skill and craftsmanship and to provide employment opportunities
9.	Uttar Pradesh	To promote industrial and economic growth in the state

Source: Various state-specific SEZ Acts and policies.

Paradoxes of the current SEZ policy

In the quest to bring about a qualitative transformation in performance of SEZs, the government came up with a set of measures to revamp EPZs in India through SEZs. To an extent, this new regime seems an improvement over the EPZ structure. However, despite various factors working in its favour and the changes initiated through economic reforms and the new trade policy (since the 1990s), the SEZ policy has been received with a fair degree of scepticism, particularly in terms of loopholes existing in the SEZ policy itself. The challenges being posed by the current SEZ policy needing a revision can be grouped under three heads: (a) the fiscal dimension of SEZs; (b) the size and location of SEZs; and (c) the approach towards factors of production.

The fiscal dimension of SEZs

Under the current SEZs regime, both the central and state governments offer a set of fiscal and non-fiscal incentives to developers, unit-holders, domestic suppliers and financial institutions engaged in these special enclaves known as Offshore Banking Units (OBUs). As against this, under the EPZs regime, incentives were offered only to exporting units. This was due to the restrictive practices followed during the EPZ period regarding the ownership and types of economic activities. Details of various exemptions and facilities provided by the central government to the developers and unit-holders under the current SEZ policy are given in Table 2.4. The major incentives offered to domestic suppliers include: (a) income tax benefit as applicable to physical export under section 80 HHC of the Income Tax Act; (b) exemption from state levies; and (c) central sales tax (CST) exemption. In addition, the SEZs include incentives to OBUs. It is, specifically, an attempt to extend financial assistance, on a priority basis, to these enclaves. It includes: (a) tax exemption under section 80LA of the Income Tax Act, 1961; (b) no separate assigned capital requirement; and (c) exemption from CRR requirements.

Table 2.4: Major Incentives Offered by the Central Government to the SEZs Developers and Unit-holders

Incentives	Developers	SEZ unit-holders
Income tax holiday	100 per cent deduction from profit derived from developing SEZs for 10 consecutive assessment years out of the first 15 years in which the SEZs are notified by the central government	Income tax holiday from the eligible profits and gains for 15 years as below: (a) 100 per cent for the first five years (b) 50 per cent for the subsequent five years (c) 50 per cent upon the creation of a specified reserve in the last five years.
Other direct tax benefits like DDT, securities transaction tax	• Exemption of DDT declared or paid after 1 April 2005 by the developer	
Central sales tax	CST exemption on all sales and purchase of goods other than newspaper	The benefit is the same as applicable to the developer
Service tax	Complete exemption from payment of service tax on all taxable services procured locally or from abroad	The benefit is the same as applicable to the developer

Incentives	Developers	SEZ unit-holders
R and D cess	Exemption from payment of R&D cess on import of technology	The benefit is the same as applicable to the developer
Custom duty	Import and export of all the goods, inputs including capital goods are exempt from the payment of custom duty – general rate being 12.5 per cent and from the applicable countervailing and/or additional custom duties	The benefit is the same as applicable to the developer
Excise duty	Exemption from the payment of excise duty on procurement of manufactured capital goods and all other inputs	The benefit is the same as applicable to the developer
Other taxes	In addition to this, the respective state governments have provided exemption from the payment of majority of state level taxes	The benefit is the same as applicable to the developer
FDI	• 100 per cent FDI allowed for township with residential, educational and recreational facilities on a case to case basis • Franchise for basic telephone service in SEZs	• 100 per cent FDI allowed under automatic route in manufacturing sector with the exception of reserved industries • No cap on foreign investment for SSI reserved items
Environment	-----	Exemption from public hearing under Environment Impact Assessment Notification
Drugs and cosmetics	-----	Exemption from port restriction under Drugs and Cosmetics Rules

Incentives	Developers	SEZ unit-holders
Sub-contracting/ contract farming	-----	• SEZ units may sub-contract part of production or production process through units in the Domestic Tariff Area or through other EOU/SEZ units • SEZ units may also sub-contract part of their production process abroad • Agriculture/ Horticulture processing SEZ units allowed to provide inputs and equipments to contract farmers in DTA to promote production of goods as per the requirement of importing countries

Source: Government of India, 2005 and 2006.

Under the state-specific policy, every state has extended tax concessions to various actors involved in the promotion, development and facilitation of SEZs. Uniformly across the states, tax exemptions are allowed in respect of local taxes and levies including sales tax, purchase tax, octroi cess etc. Due to tax constraints, if it is not advisable to grant direct exemption, the state taxes paid would be reimbursed at a later stage. A few benefits enjoyed by SEZs vary across states, as detailed in Table 2.5. For instance, in the case of electricity, a few states (Madhya Pradesh, West Bengal, Andhra Pradesh, Karnataka and Jharkhand) have extended subsidy without specifying the maximum number of years. However, in respect of Maharashtra, Orissa and Gujarat, exemption on electricity duty/tax has been extended for 10–20 years. Furthermore, there are variations observed across states with regard to giving exemption under stamp and registration duty. States like Rajasthan have defined exemption for stamp duty and registration fees very ambiguously, whereas Tamil Nadu has provided such an exemption to land alone. It would be quite interesting to locate, whether states that provide liberal incentives and subsidies have managed to improve the performance of a given zone *vis-à-vis* other states or there is any noticeable reverse trend recorded. This calls for a further research.

Table 2.5: SEZs' Incentive Structure across Major Indian States

Sl. No.	State	Incentives
1.	Uttar Pradesh	• Exemption is given for Mandi Shulka
2.	Maharashtra	• Exemption from payment of stamp duty and registration fees till 31 March 2006 • SEZs set up in C, D and D+ areas and No Industry Districts of the state have been exempted from payment of electricity duty for 15 years. However, units set up in other parts of the state have been exempted from payment of electricity duty for 10 years.
3.	Karnataka	• Exemption from entry tax for SEZ units and developers • Reduction in tax on supply of petroleum products to SEZs • Any sale of electricity to the zones should be exempted from payment of electricity tax
4.	Andhra Pradesh	• Exemption from levy of tax on entertainment held within SEZs • Exemption from levy of tax on luxuries provided within SEZs • 50 per cent exemption on payment of stamp duty and registration fee on transfer of land meant for industrial use in the SEZs • Complete exemption of stamp duty and registration fee on loan agreements, credit deeds, mortgages and hypothecation deeds executed by SEZ units for assets with SEZs in favour of banks or financial institutions will also be allowed • The state exempts SEZs from electricity duty and tax payment
5.	Tamil Nadu	• All industrial units and their expansions to be located in the SEZs will be exempt from payment of stamp duty and registration charges toward land transactions

Sl. No.	State	Incentives
6.	Rajasthan	• All industrial units and their expansions to be located in SEZs will be exempt from payment of stamp duty and registration charges • Exemption from work contract tax, entry tax, land building tax • Exemption from payment of electricity duty for SEZ developers and units that generate, transmit and distribute power for a period of 10 years from the date of commencement of such services provided that power so produced is consumed within the SEZs
7.	Orissa	• Exemption from work contract tax, entry tax, VAT, entertainment tax, luxury tax • All transfers of SEZs land in favour of strategic developers, anchors, tenants, service providers, and SEZ units would be exempt from payment of stamp duty and registration charges • Power consumed (both purchased and self-generated) in the process of development, operation and management of SEZs by SEZ developers would be exempted from payment of electricity duty/tax for a period of 20 years • Power consumed (both purchased and self-generated) by the units/establishments within SEZs would be exempted from payment of electricity duty/tax for a period of 20 years. However, there will be no exemption from payment of electricity duty/tax on the sale of power outside SEZs.
8.	Kerala	• Power generated within SEZs shall be exempted from payment of electricity duty for a period of 10 years from the date of commencement
9.	West Bengal	• 100 per cent electricity duty will be waived without any restriction in respect of all industries to be set up in Manikanchan SEZ and other SEZs

Sl. No.	State	Incentives
10.	Gujarat	• Exemption from all state taxes including sales tax, VAT, motor spirit tax, luxury tax and entertainment tax, purchase tax and other state taxes • SEZ units shall be exempted from electricity duty for 10 years from the date of production or rendering of services • Complete exemption on payment of stamp duty and registration fees for transfer of land meant for industrial use in the SEZ area (this facility to be available to both developers and unit-holders) • Complete exemption on payment of stamp duty and registration fees for loan agreements, credit deeds, mortgages etc., pertaining to SEZ units or those executed within the SEZ area
11.	Madhya Pradesh	• Exemption from all state taxes including commercial tax, turnover tax, VAT, octroi, mandi tax, purchase tax, electricity cess, stamp duty and any other such type of tax of the state government • SEZs shall be exempted from electricity duty, cess and any other tax or levy on sale of electricity for self-generated and purchased power
12.	Jharkhand	• Exemption from sales tax, VAT, luxury tax and entertainment tax and state duties on transactions within SEZs. • Exemption from sales tax and other taxes on inputs made available to SEZ units from suppliers within the state • 50 per cent exemption will be allowed for stamp duty and registration fees on transfer of lands meant for industrial use in SEZs • Complete exemption of stamp duty and registration fee for loan agreements, credit deeds, mortgages and hypothecation deeds executed by SEZs units on assets with SEZs in favour of banks or financial institutions

Source: Author's compilation based on various state-specific SEZ Acts and policies.

A critical evaluation of the various incentives offered to SEZs, however, reveals that in a bid to push them as engines of growth, the government (central/state) has placed too much emphasis on incentives. This is specifically more so because, the objective behind the promotion of SEZs in the country is based on the SEZ policy rather than the 'comparative advantage' of each state. Thus, with similar objectives and targeting of the same international clients it becomes necessary for different state governments to engage in an incentive war. Of course, the lack of incentives required for boosting the confidence of exporters was a lacuna that existed in the EPZs structure with various committees reiterating it in the 1970s and 1980s. However, this seems to have been wrongly interpreted in the present context. A glance at the incentives offered across to states under the SEZ framework gives a clear indication of the tax incentives being used as the sole strategy for attracting investors' interests. In this context, a cursory look at the literature explaining the factors shaping the export performance of a country brings out various demand and supply side factors. Until recently the policy focus in India was on the demand side, while neglecting the supply side like a well-maintained institutional set-up, infrastructural facilities, macroeconomic environment, incentives, attitude towards foreign investment and issues related to labour market. Further, at the firm level, it is factors like the size of a firm, location, availability of raw materials, technology and ownership pattern that tend to influence their performance.

On the other side, in the context of other countries, the literature on the subject lists certain factors responsible for the success or failure of such enclaves. Factors identified in the literature include the location of a given zone (Madani, 1999; Cling and Letilly, 2001; Ota, 2003), clustering and linkages with the domestic economy (Jenkins *et al.*, 1998; Jayanthakumaran, 2003), infrastructure and a supportive policy framework (Madani, 1999; Ge, 1999). Although incentives and subsidies are also considered essential for attracting investors' attention and hence are crucial to the success of zones, the empirical evidence on this issue seems inconclusive. Therefore, there is a need to concentrate on other factors from the supply side as the handicap of these factors may adversely affect the efficient working of other factors and the economy as a whole. For example, the lack of high quality infrastructure may lead to under-utilization of foreign investment as well as an increase in transport cost. In fact, a good number of industrial sectors outside the zones are contributing significantly to the generation of a trade surplus without any additional incentives. For instance, with no tax concessions on par with SEZs, the EOUs are able to contribute almost 21 per cent to the country's total trade (2008–09), thereby challenging those arguments that tax concessions offered outside the SEZs are incapable of promoting a fair level of competitiveness. The experience of China's SEZs makes it further clear that incentives are a necessary, but not a sufficient condition for boosting the performance of SEZs. The Government of China had realized this and, accordingly taken precautionary steps while extending incentives to these enclaves in terms of setting up different incentive slabs structure across zones, investor types and type of projects. At the same time, due recognition was given to other factors – infrastructural and institutional in particular as any lacunae in these factors could adversely affect the efficient working of other contributory factors as also the macro-economy. Moreover, any such incentives and subsidies may affect the government exchequer in different ways and thereby influence the distributional aspects of the budget.[11] As against the promises proposed in both the central and state-specific SEZ Acts and rules, the real claiming of incentives and benefits (both direct and indirect) is not simple. Generally, exporters find it extremely difficult to claim many such tax exemptions – largely because the actual process is very cumbersome, time-consuming and complex. In addition to this, there exists confrontation between Ministry of Commerce and Industry (MoCI) and Ministry of Finance (MoF), regarding various incentives that SEZ enterprises and developers are entitled to in real time.

Size and location of SEZs

Within 10 years of the implementation of the SEZ policy in India, the economy has seen a surge in the number of exporting units as well as fresh proposals for setting up of different types of SEZs. By March 2015, on a very large scale, 436 SEZs have been formally approved and 347 SEZs notified. The total number of operating SEZs in the country now stands at 202 (www.sezindia.nic.in).[12] It should also be noted that there is a huge gap between the number of SEZ projects approved in the country and actually operational SEZs, thereby indicating a longer gestation period involved in the realization of SEZ projects in the country. It appears that policymakers have indiscriminately approved most of the SEZ projects put before the BoA without taking into consideration the probability of their success, locational

---

11 A detailed analysis of the same is provided in chapter 5.

12 Excerpted on 7 December 2015

advantage and availability of manpower in the given regions. Moreover, as of now, no study has been undertaken by the government to analyse the problems and prospects of these upcoming SEZs. In this context, there is a need to evaluate the experience of a few zones in the country before promoting them on a large scale. Such an evaluation will be helpful in revisiting the SEZ policy against the backdrop of problems and prospects of forthcoming SEZs.

The government's approach with regard to SEZs is also in conflict with its general practice in that many development policies are first tested on an experimental basis and later, based on experience, promoted further or modified accordingly.[13] The need to stop the process of approving more SEZs gains importance, given the amount of revenue foregone by each zones.[14] In fact, the current practice of SEZ approval is found to be in variance with the practice followed in the country during the EPZ regime, in that the government acted prudently while taking decisions on the new EPZs to be set up. All the seven conventional EPZs of the country were based on the recommendations made by committees appointed for the purpose. These committees not only analysed the feasibility of setting up of new zones, but also carefully analysed the locational advantage and the products that these zones sought to promote. In fact, a couple of EPZs as proposed by the committees did not see the light of day in the late 1980s due to certain flaws in the project proposals.

An analysis of sector-wise and state-wise distribution of the formal approved SEZs brings to light a few more malpractices. Sector wise, information technology (IT)/information technology-enabled services (ITes)/electronics received maximum approvals in the country (Figure 2.1). In fact, a large part of the increase in SEZ project in the country could be attributed to the reallocation of investments from DTA to SEZs. This development is specifically noticed in the case of IT and IT-enabled industries. The prime reason for this is the introduction of the sunset clause on tax holiday for IT industry based upon the recommendations of Kelkar Committee on 'Direct and Indirect Tax Policy'. Even before Kelkar Committee, a committee headed by Dr Parthasarathi Shome also recommended the same (Palit and Bhattacharjee, 2008). Accordingly, in the 2002–03 budget, a sunset clause was set to be implemented from 31 March 2009, for Software Technology

---

13 For instance, National Rural Employment Guarantee Act (NREGA), Pradhan Mantri Adarsh Gram Yojana.

14 As elaborated in the previous section.

Park of India (STPI) and Electronic Hardware Technology Park (EHTP). Although the government attempted to nullify the argument of gradually shifting IT industry from DTA to SEZs, a quick view of the profiles of new SEZs approved by the government substantiates the counter argument that SEZs are perhaps leading the realignment of investment from DTA to SEZs, considering the fact that IT and ITes (including hardware) account for more than 60 per cent of the total approvals.

Figure 2.1: Sector-wise Distribution of SEZ Approval (Formal) in India

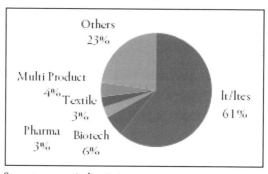

Source: www.sezindia.nic.in.

This can be seen in the failure to promote SEZs across those industries in respect of which India enjoys a comparative advantage and capability to promote employment generation; for instance, handicraft products. Instead, the maximum approvals have gone to IT industries, which do not ensure employment in a larger context in that they tend to and generate employment only for well-qualified technical workers. Thus, there is a need to give attention to other sectors as identified under the 'target approach' in the various EXIM policy statements. In this context, it is to be noted that the need for exercising caution in promoting industries had been identified way back in the early 1980s by Abid Hussain Committee (1984). Unfortunately, no thought seems to have been given to this issue; rather, decisions are taken arbitrarily regarding the approval of SEZs. At least, now, the government can think of promoting SEZs with those products in view which not only add to export performance but also impact positively the distributional aspects. Moreover, the government can also encourage SEZs for promoting those products in respect of which India enjoys an assured international market, similar to those listed in bilateral trade agreements with other countries. Such attempts can also minimize the risks associated with fluctuations in the international market and its resultant impact on these enclaves. This can be accomplished by promoting industries that are based on the 'comparative advantage' of each state/region. Moreover, the need for caution in diversifying the SEZ exports also gains importance considering their decisive role in deciding the import intensity of exports and thereby their real contribution to net foreign exchange earnings.

The promotion of SEZs based on the principle of 'comparative advantage' of each region may also help tackle regional disparities in development and thereby the problem of migration. SEZs, on the contrary, are presently concentrated in the developed states rather than underdeveloped ones in the country. For instance, developed states like Maharashtra, Andhra Pradesh, Tamil Nadu and Karnataka continue to receive more approvals, whereas other states account for only 33 per cent of the total approved SEZs in the country (Figure 2.2). Furthermore, little attention seems to have been given to the regional composition of SEZs in relation to their trade potential, i.e., little is known, as to whether zones being promoted in each state and across regions are in line with their respective comparative advantage and resource base or whether there is an arbitrary allotment of SEZ projects.

Figure 2.2: State-wise Distribution of SEZs Approvals (Formal) in India

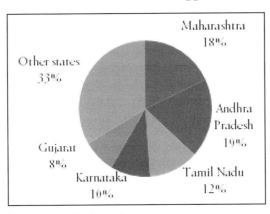

Source: www.sezindia.nic.in.

Within the developed states, SEZs are located in districts that are found to be much above the national average in terms of development parameters (Mukhopadhyay, 2009). This in turn is assumed to have adverse impact on the urban infrastructure due to congestion and diseconomies of scale (Mitra, 2007); specifically, it is feared that these zones may ruin the existing infrastructure without actually adding to the new infrastructure base in the country (Mukhopadhyay and Pradhan, 2009). Thus, SEZs may pose two types of threat towards the promotion of balanced development. Firstly, the developed states continue to receive greater share in the SEZ approval in the country vis-à-vis other states. This, in turn, may widen the already existing gap between the developed and backward states. This could be due to that regions with SEZ projects receive more attention, which, in turn deplete the resource base of the surrounding regions, thus adding more to backwash effects rather than spread effects. Second, a high concentration of SEZs in a given region tends to exhaust its resource base resulting in diseconomies of scale and congestion which, in turn, can pose a completely different set of challenges. Moreover, attempts should be made to integrate employment objectives with SEZs. This cannot be ensured merely by assigning one more objective to it, rather it calls for increased intervention on the part of the government. The most important intervention can be to make information available in employment exchange office at each zone and the units operating within each zone in order to ensure a speedy overall development. While doing so, the government can eliminate the role of middlemen besides reducing the exploitation of labour. Thus, it would be quite useful if the government could revisit the SEZ policy in this regard.

Approach towards factors of production

In the current SEZ structure, labour-related powers are transferred from the state labour commissioner to the development commissioner of the respective zones. This is aimed at providing a hassle-free business environment, specifically to avoid all types of labour unrest. Furthermore, despite the provision made in the SEZs Act, the real practice with regard to the exercising labour-related powers varies significantly across the seven conventional zones. Across zones, four different types of arrangements have been noticed in respect of managing labour-related issues. Development commissioners, by law, exercise the powers of labour commissioner in Kandla, Santacruz, Noida and Vizag SEZs, whereas in the case of Falta SEZ, the state labour commissioner exercises control over labour-related issues. The development commissioner of Chennai SEZ has voluntarily handed over powers to the state labour commissioner to deal with labour-related issues, but occasionally oversees the work of the latter. In the case of Cochin SEZ, the development commissioner has been provided with inspection officers to handle labour issues within the zone and accordingly he/she assigns the state labour commissioner the task of dealing with labour issues. However, the above arrangement is not in conformity with the provisions of the SEZ Acts and thereby reveals an apparent inconsistency between the real practice and the actual provision made in the SEZ policy.

Moreover, the SEZ Act fails to realize the possible mismatch between demand for and supply of labour either in absolute or in relative terms and as such, fails to establish the source of labour force. The labour market is assumed to be supplying the required work force. However, in practice, across the seven zones it is observed that the labour market has failed to meet the specific requirements, leaving scope for the entry of middlemen and subsequently the exploitation of workers. Thus, there is a need for government intervention to ensure the supply of manpower to these zones and thereby avoid any form of labour exploitation. In fact, SEZs can be used as an effective tool for improving the skill formation of the youth through vocational education training so as to make them more employable. This, in turn, can help improve human resource development of the economy.

Furthermore, land-related issues are ignored in the current structure, that is, it is silent on issues related to the acquisition of land, the compensation formula, etc. Considering that the government does not have sufficient land in its possession to be allotted for the development of all SEZs, acquiring land from private owners either on lease basis or through purchase is the only viable option. Under the circumstances a few questions emerge – how will the private land be acquired? Who is authorized to acquire? What type of private land can be acquired? More importantly, how much will these private owners get as compensation and what should be the criteria for deciding the compensation?

In the absence of any explanation in this respect in SEZ Act, initially, the respective state governments were acquiring land from private owners under the banner of public purpose as defined in the Land Acquisition Act, 1894. This was basically due to the ambiguity in defining what constitutes public utility service (Kasturi, 2008). With respect to this, there are divergent views also as to who should acquire land for SEZs development. Bhaduri (2007) strongly advocates negotiation between the private actor and the landowner to rule out the possibility of government intervention. A few (Banerjee *et al.*, 2007; Bose, 2007), however, strongly support active government involvement considering the pitfalls in direct negotiations. The government, while taking a cautious approach, declared 5 April 2007, as the cut-off point for land acquisition and accordingly the BoA set a few guidelines for granting SEZ approvals.[15] Moreover, the real practice of state intervention in land acquisition differs across major Indian states. For instance, in Tamil Nadu in view of a huge land bank in its possession before the enactment of SEZ Act in the state, the government did not face any set back in dealing with land-related issues, while promoting SEZs.[16] Furthermore, in the absence of a well-defined rehabilitation and resettlement policy, the initial years also saw debates over the criteria for defining compensation. Generally, it is defined by the government based on the current market price, which is again questionable considering the practice of under-reporting in respect of land deeds and sales to save on stamp duties (Gill, 2007; Kasturi, 2008). Even if it is above the market price, inflation further brings down the compensation value (Gill, 2007). Thus, alternative models are suggested in the literature. A few argue in favour of monthly pension along with savings bonds (Gill, 2007) and employment assurance for one person from each family. Mukhopodhyay (2009), however, proposes transfer of part of the profits from successful SEZ projects to a community fund, to be used for the development of physical and social infrastructure in a given region. Related to this, there is the issue of who should be compensated in the process of land acquisition. As per the provision in the Land Acquisition Act 1894, compensation is to be paid only to landowners and non-landowners such as tillers, tenants and agricultural labourers, and women are not eligible. The government has taken initiatives to address this issue by placing the National Rehabilitation and Resettlement Policy for approval in Parliament.[17] Despite such a timely intervention,

---

15 For a discussion, see Menon and Mitra (2009).

16 See, for a discussion on this, Vijayabhaskar (2010).

17 Of late, there has been attempt to revise the age-old land acquisition and resettlement bills. First one is seen under the United Progressive Alliance (UPA) government in the year 2013. Accordingly, the Right to Fair Compensation and Transparency in Land Acquisition, Rehabilitation and Resettlement Act, 2013 came into existence. On the positive side, as per this, focuses on providing not only compensation to the land owners, but also extends rehabilitation and resettlement benefits to livelihood looser from the land, which shall be in addition to the minimum compensation. On the negative side, it has some serious shortcomings as regards to its provisions for socio-economic impact assessment and it also bypassed the constitutional local self governments by not recognizing them as 'appropriate governments' in matters of land acquisition. The second amendment is proposed by the current National Democratic Alliance (NDA)-led government and presently it is still debated.

the issue of displacement caused by such development projects is yet to be resolved, specifically considering the experiences in Nandigram SEZ project in West Bengal, Mangalore SEZ in Karnataka and Jamnagar SEZ project in Gujarat. Moreover, issues like how to distribute the expected benefits from such projects to different stakeholders involved in the process are yet to be resolved. Furthermore, the spread of SEZs in the country has also been questioned in terms of the possible implications for the state of agriculture and future food security (Shah, 2010). Unlike China, SEZs in India are not confined to any specific region and are spread all over the country. In short, the problems associated with the liberal promotion of SEZs in the country are likely to persist in the future, unless corrective measures are undertaken in the meanwhile.

Summary

On the basis of the above analysis, we argue that the failure of the EPZ structure in making its mark on the Indian economy was mainly due to policy failure, that is, there was no well-articulated policy in place that could accommodate and execute the factors necessary for their success. This could be seen in the loopholes existing in the pre-reform period policy. As aptly noted by Grasset and Landy (2007), the strong presence of the License Raj system and the difficulties involved in accessing imports and exports made EPZs less attractive. Nevertheless, at the implementation level, a prudent approach was followed not only in choosing the number of zones to be set up in the country, but also in locating these zones. Although the early 1990s witnessed changes in the operation and working definition of EPZs, in line with the government efforts in terms of revamping the economic structure as part of economic reforms, but a few structural issues were overlooked even in the second phase. For instance, the role of state-specific agendas and the importance of decentralization were not recognized.

It was in the first decade of economic reforms that a radical move was noticed in terms of imitating the Chinese model of SEZs. Nevertheless, the imitation of the Chinese model of trade policy in the country seems an improvement over the conventional EPZs, thereby fulfilling its promise of promoting qualitative transformation of EPZs. The current SEZ policy is also known for its clarity in objectives, a broader economic area to operate and the recognition of the role of different actors in the promotion of SEZs. Despite numerous positives associated with it, the SEZ policy in India needs a pragmatic re-visit. Specifically, the current SEZ policy seems to be suffering from flaws in the ideas behind policy formulation and also at the execution level. The most important argument in its favour stems from the various flaws in the policy, which is in conflict with other development objectives of the economy. The major ones are the government's stand on incentives offered to different actors involved in the process, land acquisition and compensation formulae and the sectoral and geographical expansion of SEZs in the country. Thus, as a way ahead, we argue that there is a need for restructuring the SEZ scheme in the country in terms of identifying the problems and prospects associated with expansion rather than just extending liberal incentive packages.

Annexure

Annexure Table 2.1: Chronology of Major Policy Developments in the Evolution of EPZs/SEZs in India

(1960–2012)

Year	Policy initiatives
Policy intervention in the first phase of EPZs regime (1960–90)	
1958	The early thought of creating FTZs in western coastal India
1961	Lok Sabha approved the decision of promoting an FTZ in Kandla, India
1965	The establishment of an FTZ in Kandla
1966–67	Kandla FTZ (KAFTZ) became operational
1967–72	Number of concessions were offered to attract investment in the zone
1972	The establishment of Santacruz EPZ for the export of electronics products
1973–74	Santacruz EPZ became operational
1978–84	The government constituted several committees for trade promotion and these committees offered numerous recommendations for improving the structure and performance of these enclaves. • Committee to look into the problems hindering the growth of KAFTZ (1978) • Alexander Committee on Import and Export Policies (1978) • Review Committee on Electronics (1979) • Dagli Committee on Controls and Subsidies (1979) • Tondon Committee on Export Strategy (1980) • Committee on FTZs and 100 per cent EOUs (1982) • Abid Husain Committee on Trade policy (1984)
1980	DTA sale is permitted up to 25 per cent of production against import license on payment of applicable custom duties Sale of rejects up to 5 per cent allowed on payment of applicable duties Disposal of waste and scrap allowed on payment of applicable custom/excise duties Sub-contracting of production process/part of production permitted for EPZ units with the approval of Commissioner of Customs

Year	Policy initiatives
1981	Five-year tax holiday granted to EPZ units
1986	Reimbursement of central sales tax to EPZ units Gems and jewellery sector given permission to operate in SEEPZ
1984	The decision to establish EPZs in Cochin, Chennai, Falta and Noida was approved
1985–86	EPZs in Cochin, Chennai, Falta and Noida started functioning
1987	DTA sale permitted up to 25 per cent of production on payment of full custom duties EOUs granted five year tax holiday and reimbursement of CST
1988	Sub-contracting of production process/part of production permitted for EOUs with the approval of Commissioner of Customs
1989	The decision to establish Vizag EPZ was approved
Policy intervention in the second phase of the EPZ regime (1990–2000)	
1991	DTA sale permitted up to 25 per cent of production on payment of 50 per cent of custom duties
1992	The agriculture, horticulture and aquaculture sectors allowed to operate under the umbrella of EPZs/EOUs
1994	DTA sale permitted up to 50 per cent in the case of agro-products on payment of 50 per cent of custom duties. Sub-contracting of production process/part of production permitted for EPZ units with the approval of the Assistant Commissioner of Customs concerned Trading, re-engineering and reconditioning units were also permitted to be set up within EPZs Vizag EPZ became operational
1995	Disposal of waste and scrap allowed on payment of 50 per cent of applicable customs/excise duty
	Sale of rejects up to 5 per cent allowed on 50 per cent of applicable duties

Year	Policy initiatives
1997	Disposal of waste and scrap allowed on payment of applicable excise duty in case waste and scrap have been generated wholly from indigenous raw materials; otherwise duty to be leviable at 50 per cent of customs or excise duty, whichever is high.
	Sub-contracting of production process/part of production (a) Approval to be given by development commissioner for final processing by customs; (b) Units using predominantly indigenous raw materials allowed to subcontract part of production in the DTA
	DTA sale (a) Permitted up to 25 per cent of production on payment of 50 per cent of customs duty or excise duty, whichever is high. (b) Permitted on payment of excise duty in the case of goods produced wholly from indigenous raw materials. (c) Additional DTA sale over and above 25 per cent of production in respect of freely importable goods on payment of full duties subject to achievement of VA and meeting export obligations. (d) Electronics hardware units allowed to sell up to 50 per cent of production on payment of full duty without linkage with VA achieved. (e) Permitted software units outline DTA sale.
1998–99	Promotional measures/procedural changes announced like • extension of tax holiday for EOUs/EPZs to 10 years; • sub-contracting facility for DTA; • permission to set up private software technology parks;
1999–2000	FTZs to be replaced EPZs and these were to be treated as outside the country's exports. Entitlement of DTA sales for EOUs and EPZs increased to 50 per cent of f.o.b. value of the previous year. NFE as a per cent of exports made uniform at 20 per cent for both EOUs and EPZs .

Year	Policy initiatives
	Policy initiatives during the SEZ regime (2000 onwards)
2000–01	All existing EPZs were converted into SEZs, as per the focus of the EXIM Policy Statement of 1997–2002. Announced on 1 April 2000.
	The sale of tea by Export Oriented Units (EOUs) and units in EPZs in Domestic Tariff Area (DTA) was banned.
	With a view to simplifying the operating regime, SEZs, EPZs and EOUs were exempted from industrial licensing requirement for the establishment of projects for manufacture of items reserved for the small scale sector.
	The units within SEZs were permitted to credit 100 per cent of their foreign exchange receipts to EEFC accounts except foreign exchange acquired by way of purchase against rupees from any resident of India other than another unit in a SEZ
	The Union Budget for 2001–02 announced the following major policies for safeguarding the interests of domestic producers in the context of a proposed complete removal of QRs for boosting exports:
	• A 10 year tax holiday for the developers of SEZs on the same lines as developers of industrial parks
	• A provision to exempt anti-dumping duty or safeguarding duty on goods imported by 100 per cent EOUs, units within the free trade zones or SEZs
	With respect to SEZs, foreign direct investment (FDI) was permitted under automatic route for all manufacturing sectors, except a small negative list.
	The SEZs developers were allowed duty free import/procurement from DTA for the development of SEZs with a view to giving to a boost to development of integrated infrastructure for exports.
	The units within SEZs were allowed to bring back their proceeds in 365 days and retain 100 per cent of proceeds in exchange earners' foreign currency (EEFC) account.
	The SEZ developers would be made eligible for various entitlements as provided for in the Income Tax Act.
	To speed up the approval process, the government constituted a single BoA for EPZs/SEZs/EOUs as a matter of procedural simplification.

Year	Policy initiatives
2001–02	To speed up the approval process, the government constituted a single BoA for EPZs/SEZs/EOUs towards procedural simplification. The EXIM Policy Statement of 2002–07 provided certain exemptions for units operating within SEZS. It includes: • OBUs permitted to be set up in SEZs which, *inter alia*, would be exempt from CRR, SLR and give SEZ units and SEZ developers access to international finance at international rates. • Income tax concessions would be given to units operating within SEZs. • Exemption from Central Sales Tax (CST) to supplies from (DTA) domestic tariff area to SEZs. • Drawback/Duty Entitlement Pass Book (DEPB) to DTA suppliers. • Transactions from DTA to SEZs would be treated as exports under Income Tax Act and Customs Act. • Exemption to SEZ units from external commercial borrowings (ECB) restrictions, freedom to make overseas investment and carry out commodity hedging. The Union Budget of 2002–03 further provided certain incentives to units working within SEZs. It includes: • 100 per cent deduction of export profits under Section 10A to all SEZ units commencing production on or after 1 April 2002, for a period of five years, and thereafter at 50 per cent for the next two years. • Supplies to SEZs from DTA to be treated as physical exports instead of deemed exports for the purposes of duties, tariffs and central sales tax. At present, a person resident in India is prohibited from taking any general or life insurance policy issued by an insurer outside India. It was decided, in consultation with Government of India, to exempt units located within SEZs from the purview of the above stipulations for taking out general insurance policies. Accordingly, Ads are free to allow remittances towards premium for general insurance policies taken by units located within SEZs from insurers outside India provided the premium is paid by the units out of their foreign exchange balances. Extension of the concessions available for infrastructure by way of a 10-year tax holiday to the developers of SEZs on the same lines as developers of industrial parks.

Year	Policy initiatives
	Setting up of agri-economic zones to promote agricultural exports on the basis of specific products and specific geographical areas.
	SEZs have been liberalized further by granting permission to SEZ developers for duty free import/procurement from DTA, to sell goods in the DTA in accordance with the import duty in force, for subcontracting a part of production abroad, to bring back their export proceeds in 365 days (as against the normal period of 180 days) and to retain 100 per cent of the proceeds in the EEFC account and introducing measures such as no requirement of license for setting up units in these zones for items reserved for SSI and granting of infrastructure status, under the Income Tax Act, to SEZ developers.
	Additional benefits to EOU/EPZ/EHTP/STP units include rationalization of NFEP/EP norms; supplies made by the trading units to the bonded warehouses to be treated as exports for the purpose of domestic sales entitlement; sub-contracting of production abroad permitted; simplification of procedures regarding the utilization of goods and a greater delegation of power to development commissioners for approving EOU/EPZ projects.
2002–03	Units located in SEZs are allowed to open, hold and maintain foreign currency accounts with an authorized dealer in India subject to certain conditions, in lieu of the special provision for EEFC accounts for units in the SEZs given earlier.
	The RBI formulated a scheme for the setting up of OBUs in SEZs by commercial banks.
	Entities in the SEZs granted general permission to undertake hedging transactions in the international commodity exchanges/markets to hedge their commodity price risk on import/export, provided such transactions are undertaken on 'stand-alone' basis.
	A separate export promotion council for EOUs and units of SEZs set up to enhance exports by these entities. It would function as an approved trade body like other export promotion councils and facilitate the functioning of the units concerned.
	A number of incentives/facilities for SEZs were announced: • The stipulation of 12 months or an extended period thereof for realization of export proceeds was removed in respect of SEZs. • Units in SEZs permitted to undertake job work abroad and export goods from that country itself, subject to certain conditions.

Year	Policy initiatives
	• Gems and jewellery units in SEZs and EOUs allowed to receive payments for exports in the form of precious metals, that is, gold/silver/platinum equivalent to the value of jewellery exported, subject to certain conditions.
	• Netting off export receivables against import payments as well as capitalization of import payables permitted, subject to stipulated conditions for SEZ units.
	Units for the generation and distribution of powers permitted within SEZs, to ease power-related issues in and around SEZs.
2003–04	Units in SEZs allowed to raise ECBs in compliance with the guidelines issued by the Government of India, subject to the conditions that they (i) raise ECBs for their own requirement; and (ii) not transfer on-lending any borrowed funds to their sister concerns or any other units in DTA.
2004–05	All supplies made to SEZs to be treated as physical exports with effect from 1 September 2004 and entitled for benefits of Duty-Free Replenishment Certificate (DFRC) under the foreign trade policy.
	As per the existing guidelines, nominated agencies/approved banks can import gold on loan basis for on-lending to exporters of jewellery and by EOUs and units in SEZs for manufacturing and export of jewellery on their own account only. After a review of these guidelines, the maximum tenor of gold loan was enhanced to 240 days, that is, 60 days for manufacture and export, and 180 days for fixing the price and repayments. ADs permitted to open standby LCs for tenor equivalent to the loan period and on behalf of entities permitted to import gold. The standby LC should be in favour of the internationally renowned bullion banks only.
	SEZ units obtaining gold/silver/platinum from the nominated agencies on loan basis required to export that jewellery within 90 days from the date of release, except outright purchase.
2005-06	SEZ Act 2005 passed in the parliament.
	Supplies from domestic tariff area (DTA) to SEZs made eligible for benefits under Duty Free Entitlement Certificate.
	(DFEC) and Target Plus Scheme subject to the specified conditions, provided the payments are realized in free foreign exchange.
	In exercise of the powers conferred by Section 55 of the Special Economic Zone Act, 2005 (28 of 2005), the central government announced SEZs rules, 2006 containing definitions, procedures, etc., regarding setting up and operation of SEZs.

Year	Policy initiatives
2006–07	SEZs Rule, 2006 came in to force. First SEZs Amendment Rules, 2006 was introduced.
2007–08	Second SEZ Amendment Rules, 2006 was introduced. Its major components include: • Minimum land requirements for development of different types of SEZs revised • Minimum processing area requirements rationalized and revised (25–35–50 per cent) • Directions for provision of specified type of infrastructure (e.g., 24/7 power, AC) • Bar on the use of previously used plant and machinery • Empowering the BoA to relax contiguity criteria, allowing changes in the categorization of SEZs • Reduction of validity period of in-principle approval (one year, extendable by one year at a time) • Procedural changes – introduction of new forms, approval letters, etc.
2008–09	Authorized dealers allowed for SEZ developers to open, hold and maintain EEFC accounts and to credit up to 100 per cent of their foreign exchange earnings.
2009–10 onwards	Hazardous Wastes Management, Handling and Transboundary Movement Third Amendment Rules, 2010 came into existence. Exemption to SEZ developers from obtaining distribution licence. Respective development commissioners of the jurisdictional SEZs to be the enforcement officers in respect of the notified offences committed in a SEZ. Sections 20–22 of the SEZs Act 2005 came into force.

Source: Review Committee on Electronics (1979), IIFT (1990), Kundra (2000); Reserve Bank of India Annual Report, various issues, EXIM Policy statement of various years, various issues of Economic Survey of India.

3

China's Experience with Special Economic Zones under a Liberalized Regime – Highs and Lows

Background

The articulation of a hard-nosed policy with respect to SEZs is of special significance among the various measures introduced by the Deng Xiaoping government, to liberalize the external sector of the Chinese economy. Although this policy shift among others was aimed at testing seeds of capitalism (Zeng, 2011) within a rigid socialistic framework, once set up, these economic enclaves began acting as prime engines of the economic transformation of China in the post-reform period, and subsequently, gained worldwide attention and even widespread emulation. Apparently, a few economies that were keen observers of the development path of China's economic reform, including India,[1] tried to replicate similar reform strategies. However, the replication of the Chinese model of SEZs in the Indian context led to certain set backs, raising questions regarding the appropriateness of experimenting such a measure.[2] In fact, the concept of SEZs in India was received with more scepticism than expectations in India. In this context, it becomes imperative to ask and understand why and how a certain policy implementation that was stunningly successful in one country turned out to be incapable of meeting the expectations upon its emulation in another. This requires a two-pronged approach: (a) to understand the conceptual rigor, pragmatic tenor and a flawless implementation of the SEZ

---

1   In 2008, Pakistan also followed a similar line of reforms by way of introducing SEZs.

2   Literature pertaining debate on current SEZ policy of India has already been discussed in chapter 1.

policy in China before delineating carefully the factors that allowed and even facilitated such an implementation; and (b) to analyse, in retrospect, the SEZ expansion trajectory in the context of Chinese economy in addition to addressing issues such as the effectiveness of SEZs in transforming a traditional economy into a modern one and quantifying the challenges and economic set backs of SEZ expansion in China. Thus, an exploration along the following these lines, is crucial to understanding the success story of SEZs in China: (a) to identify factors contributing to the success of the Chinese SEZ policy, as also various supportive mechanisms, both internal and external, that have played an important role in scripting this success story; (b) to identify the inadequacies in the way Indian policymakers understood the demands underlying such a policy shift and its implementation, and also the institutional and infrastructural requirements that should have been provided for its emulation; and (c) to identify the lessons that India can imbibe in its attempt to redefine the SEZ policy, which, doubtless, has become a necessity now.

For an in-depth study, among the five full-fledged SEZs and 14 ETDZs of China, we chose Shenzhen SEZ for two reasons. First, given its size, Shenzhen SEZ represents a classic case of an industrial township. Second, its commanding performance according to the stated objectives relative to other SEZs and its transformation from a small fishing community to a full-fledged industrial township makes it worthy of study. The reference period of the study spanned three decades from 1980 to 2012–13. The analysis is based on various policy documents related to Chinese SEZs, secondary data (*Chinese Statistical Year Book*, 2012 and *Shenzhen Statistical Year Book*, 2006 and 2013) and the author's extended fieldwork in China.[3]

The underpinnings of China's policy on SEZs[4]

In the late 1970s, SEZs were proposed as an integral measure towards reforming the external sector of the Chinese economy. Notwithstanding a

---

3 The fieldwork was carried out in 2007 (across two cities of China, namely Beijing and Shenzhen) and 2013 (across three cities of China, namely Beijing, Chegadu and Shanghai).

4 Originally published in *India Quarterly: A Journal of International Affairs*, Vol. 68, No. 3 Copyright © 2012 Indian Council of World Affairs (ICWA). All rights reserved. Reproduced with the permission of the copyright holders and the publishers, Sage Publications India Pvt. Ltd, New Delhi. However, substantial changes have been made in this section.

number of ordinances and circulars issued by both the central and respective local governments towards promoting these enclaves, it was the 'Regulation of the Peoples Republic of China on Special Economic Zone' passed in 1980 that provided a legal framework for the creation and operation of SEZs in China. In this section, we present the various components of the SEZ policy in China, in order to explain how Chinese policymakers meticulously introduced various reform measures required for the promotion and success of SEZs.

The concept

Undoubtedly, the origin of the concept of SEZs dates back to the early nineteenth century, though under different nomenclatures,[5] but the Chinese economy took the credit for popularizing the term 'Special Economic Zone'. It was introduced as an experimental tool to test the possible implications of injecting the market forces into a centrally planned and controlled economy. At a cursory glance, it seems to be a replication of the Asian export processing zones. However, a closer scrutiny of the same reveals that the Chinese SEZ are a revised and enlarged version of EPZs not only in terms of geographical size but also in terms of spatial spread, policies, incentives, institutional structure, management and coverage of economic activities.[6] This implicitly justifies the term 'special' in its terminology as well as help to locate how different these enclaves are not only within China, but also in comparison to their counterparts in other countries. For instance, SEZs were perceived as 'windows and radiators' (Ge, 1999) of the economic reforms of China. As 'windows' to the outside world, they were expected to disseminate the dimensions of world market and to promote technology transfer, whereas, as 'radiators', they were aimed at establishing linkages between SEZs and other sectors in the country. These enclaves were also perceived as an economic bridge between foreigners and the Chinese (Wall, 1993). Article 1 of the 'Regulation of the Peoples Republic of China on Special Economic Zone' provides a clear illustration of the objectives in the promotion of SEZs in China, whereas Article 4 outlines the economic activities permitted in such zones:

> Certain areas are delineated from the three cities of Guangdong
> Province to form SEZ to promote economic cooperation and

---

5   See World Bank (1992), for details on the evolution of the concept of SEZ.

6   A detailed explanation of each of these is given in the subsequent subsection.

technical exchanges with foreign countries and to encourage the socialist modernization programme

(Article 1 of Regulation of the Peoples Republic of China on Special Economic Zone)

... Investors may establish, with their own investment or in joint ventures with our side, all projects that have positive significance for international economic cooperation and technical exchanges ,including industry, agriculture, animal husbandry, aquaculture, tourism, housing and construction, and research and manufacture involving high technology, as well as other businesses of common interest to investors and to our side.

(Article 4 of Regulation of the Peoples Republic of China on Special Economic Zone)

Variants of development zones in China and their locations

Other than SEZs, Chinese policymakers did indeed experiment with alternative typologies of development zones, while taking into account problems and prospects of each region. Initially, four SEZs were set up, one each in Shenzhen, Zuhai, Shantou (in Guangdong Province) and Xiamen (in Fujian Province). Through SEZs, the government targeted the development of a particular sector in each enclave (Ramachandran and Cletus, 1999). For instance, instead of getting too ambitious about the implementation of the SEZ policy, the process of industrialization in Shenzhen was introduced gradually in three stages (Wong and Chu, 1985). Initially, considering the inherent advantages and difficulties in the region, an emphasis was placed on small-scale industries, especially labour-intensive modern industries. This approach was quite helpful in increasing employment opportunities in this region. In the second stage, there was a special emphasis on advanced technology-based industries. In the third stage, the industrial base of the region was diversified: specifically, by setting up advanced technology-based industries with modern scientific methods of production. This phase-wise approach was helpful in developing the infrastructure base in the region in a systematic manner without inviting much of a fiscal burden, and also to a great extent, in facilitating the spread of production technology across the domestic enterprises. Subsequently, based on the successful experience of the initial four SEZs, different typologies of such developmental zones were introduced in the other coastal regions of the country. Accordingly, 14 coastal regions were opened up for foreign trade and investment in 1984.[7] In addition, 15 free trade zones, 32 state-level economic and technological development zones and 53 new- and high-tech industrial development zones were established in large- and medium-sized cities, as a way of attracting technology-intensive and export-oriented industries. Hainan Island was given the status of a province in 1988, and subsequently, it emerged as the fifth SEZ of China. Shanghai was given the status of 'open area' in 1990 and, in the subsequent years, 10 other major inland cities were opened up. Recently, Shanghai has been accorded the status of a free trade zone. Altogether, the Chinese government experimented with different types of reform measures so as to liberalize the external sector of the economy, by taking advantage of the geographic and development prospects of each region. In addition, there were differences between these zones in terms of geographical size, incentive structure and administrative control. SEZs were given a more liberal set of incentives besides being provided with an investment friendly environment as compared to ETDZs and open areas. This broadly corresponds to the different generations of reform in the administration and maintenance of these zones in China.

With regard to location, a very prudent approach was followed for identifying and designating the development zones across specific regions of China. Among the eight coastal provinces of China at that time, Guangdong and Fujian provinces, which were chosen for setting up the initial four SEZs, had lagged far behind in terms of economic strength, industrial development and commercialization (Ng and David, 1985). From this, it is evident that the economic factors were not the only important ones with respect to the selection and that the social and ethnic factors also had played a significant role in the location of zones (ibid), specifically for targeting the overseas Chinese residing in Hong Kong, Macau and Taiwan.[8] Hence, the policy of SEZ in

---

7   This includes Dalian, Qinhuangdao, Tianjin, Yantai, Qingdao, Lianyungang, Nantong, Shanghai, Ningbo, Wenzhou, Fuzhou, Guangzhou, Zhanjiang and Beihai (Bahl, 1996). Following this, in 1985, the Chinese Government decided to expand the open coastal areas, by extending the open economic zones of the Yangtze River Delta, Pearl River Delta and Xiamen-Zhangzhou-Quanzhou Triangle in South Fujian; Shandong Peninsula, Liaodong Peninsula, Hebei and Guangxi into an open coastal belt.

8   In fact, in a recent study, it is argued that SEZs in Shenzhen, since 1990s, have played an active role in shaping the Hong Kong economy (Yeung et al., 2009).

China was also used as a strategy to take advantage of the nationalistic spirit of non-resident Chinese, while combining it with a broader national economic policy. This objective of the government had been clearly spelt out in Article 1 of the Rules (1980) governing SEZs in Guangdong and other provinces. Among the five SEZs, Shenzhen is closer to Hong Kong (36 km off from Hong Kong), Zuhai is near Macau, Shantou happens to be the hometown of most overseas Chinese, and Xiamen SEZ (in Fujian Province) is closely linked to Taiwan (see Table 3.1). A similar approach was followed while locating the fifth SEZ in China at Hainan as well as in the case of other ETDZs and open areas in Shanghai. Such an approach enabled these regions to revive and nurture the industrial culture of neighbouring regions by attracting nearby overseas investors and subsequently diffusing across the rest of China.

Geographically, all these typologies of development zones were located closer to the coastal regions of south and southeast China, with a view to providing port facilities needed for promoting and expanding trade activities (See Map 3.1), and, thereby, bringing about a reduction in the transport costs involved in trade promotion. Notably, these regions were given special facilities with liberal incentive structures at a time when other parts of China were still under a rigid control of the Chinese centralized planning system. This policy of the Chinese authorities represented 'one country dual policy' principle. Therefore, a deeper exploration of this dual policy is very crucial in understanding and evaluating China's economic reforms.

Table 3.1: A Basic Profile of the Chinese SEZs

Sl. No	SEZs	Province	Before SEZ	Inherent advantages	Administration
1.	Shenzhen (1979)	Guangdong	A small village with fisheries as the major occupation	Near Hong Kong city Access to port	It was independent of the province to which it now belongs.
2.	Zuhai (1979)	Guangdong	Underdeveloped	Nearby Macau It had a long tradition in international relations.	Controlled by the provincial government

Sl. No	SEZs	Province	Before SEZ	Inherent advantages	Administration
3.	Shantou (1979)	Guangdong	It already had an established industrial centre.	It was home of many Chinese emigrants.	It was independent of the province to which it now belongs.
4.	Xiamen (1979)	Fujian	It was a trading centre.	It had a long history of trade ties with Taiwan.	It was independent of the province to which it now belongs.
5.	Hainan (1984)	Hainan	It was underdeveloped in terms of an industrial base and infrastructural facilities.	It had a good natural resource base that was almost exclusively shipped to the mainland.	Controlled by the provincial government

Source: Author's compilation.

Map 3.1: Location of SEZs and ETDZs in China

Source: http://www.lib.utexas.edu/maps/china.html.

Focus on supply side factors

At the time of initiating economic reforms, China had better demand side factors. For instance, the rules of the game related to the international trade were very minimal. In fact, when China initiated its liberalization process, there was no World Trade Organization (WTO) and its regulations. Such an environment gave a lot of scope to experiment with policy measures. Second, China hardly had any competitor in the international market, at least in East Asia. Moreover, there was a strong presence of overseas investors in its neighbouring countries. Given such a conducive environment, the success of economic reforms was largely dependent on the internal policy measures in terms of addressing inadequacies that existed in pre-reform China. At this juncture, the government's conscious approach towards reforming three 'Is' evidently influenced the transition process of the Chinese economy through SEZs; these three 'Is' related to institutional structure (administrative procedures), incentive schemes and infrastructure arrangements, as a mechanism to address these supply side constraints. These are discussed here in detail.

Changes in the institutional (administrative) arrangements

One of the striking features of the Chinese system, *vis-à-vis* capitalist countries, is its political set-up, governed by socialist ideology (Narayanan, 2006). This aspect has shaped the reform agenda of China. Unlike democratic countries, in China, the Communist Party wields an absolute power with a strong knowledge-based cadre. Prior to the reforms period, all economic decisions in China were determined by a centralized planning body that was mainly characterized by the sluggish and inefficient bureaucratic procedures. Moreover, the state-run enterprises dominated the industrial sector with complete control over production, import and export of goods (Lardly, 2005). As a result, hardly any competition was faced from either private or foreign origin companies, which eventually affected resource allocation, utilization and, consequently, the pace of economic growth and the composition of China's foreign trade. This, in particular, could be seen in China's engagement in the production and export of those commodities in respect of which it had neither comparative advantages nor producers with any incentives to expand production owning to the centralized planning system (Lardly, 2005). Besides, despite having an abundant surplus labour force, China focused on producing capital-intensive products. Furthermore, the Chinese Government considered its hold on land and labour as a means of maintaining its control over the masses (Wall, 1993). These three components – centralized planning, dominance of the state-owned enterprises (SOE) and the rigid labour and land markets – were the prime impediments to China's economic progress in the pre-reform period. The SEZ policy became handy for rectifying these countervailing conditions as well as for trying out an alternative system of administration; it also marked the beginning of economic decentralization in China in addition to breaking the long tradition of a centrally planned model of administration. The decentralization process introduced as part of economic reforms in general has had far reaching implications for the Chinese economy in three ways (Li, 2004). First, owing to an increased autonomy of the decision making process, the local-level governments became actively interested in the enclaves' performance in the same way as the central government. Second, the arrangement of sharing revenue between the local- and higher-level governments also acted as an incentive for the former to take additional care for improving the performance of economic actors under their control. Third, the division of resources and economic activities at different layers of government enabled the local governments to effectively distribute time and resources towards enhancing the performance levels.

With respect to SEZs, the decentralization process was implemented through Article 24 of 'The Regulation of the Peoples Republic of China on Special Economic Zone', under which SEZs were brought directly under the control of local provincial committees, thereby enabling them to enjoy vast powers in terms of administration, management, promotion and maintenance of SEZs. In the case of Shenzhen SEZ, it was brought under the administration of Guangdong Provincial Committee. Similar offices were set up in Shantou, Zuhai and Xiamen. All these five SEZs were also independent of local government rules and regulations, but were integrated with a broader national policy (Hameed, 1996). In addition, Shenzhen and Hainan were vested with special powers to formulate separate laws to promote and achieve the objectives of SEZs in their respective regions, subject to their being consistent with the national policies. Guangdong Provincial Committee, for instance, enjoyed the following jurisdictional powers with respect to the management of its SEZs.

- Formulating and implementing development plans for the special zones
- Examining and approving various investment projects of the zones
- Handling the registration of industrial and commercial enterprises of the special zones

- Dealing with land allotment in the special zones
- Facilitating coordinative working relations among the banking, insurance, taxation, customs, frontier inspection, postal and telecommunications and other organizations in the special zones
- Administering labour-specific issues like providing the required labour force to enterprises in the special zones and protecting the legitimate rights and interests of workers
- Maintaining law and order in the special zones

(Article 23 of Regulation of the People's Republic of China on Special Economic Zone)

These apart, local governments were empowered to take decisions with regard to either reducing or exempting surtax payable by foreign funded enterprises (Kundra, 2000). In a nutshell, the decentralization of power has had a greater impact on the overall functioning of SEZs in China, specifically in breaking the dominance of centralized planning and administration at the sub-national levels, which in a way hampered the efficiency of the administrative structure prevalent earlier.

Incentives as a tool to attract investor confidence

Given the rigid Communist government practices, China had hardly attracted any attention from either foreign or domestic investors at the time of initiating reforms. Therefore, it was quite necessary for the government to publicize the new economic policy as well as the liberalized business environment in China. The incentive structure became an instrument of choice for the promotion of SEZs in China, and for this purpose, various fiscal and non-fiscal incentives were offered,[9] though at the same time, a very restrictive investment environment continued to exist in other parts of China. The incentives offered to enterprises within SEZs, however, varied across zones depending on the type of industries targeted for promotion in each zone. Furthermore, by 1984, the government had come up with different slabs of incentives applicable to various projects and particularly higher incentives were extended to those joint ventures which assured new technology transfers and/or higher investments (Oborne, 1986). Needless to add, the incentive packages followed were also flexible in nature.

---

9   See Annexure Table 3.1, for a detailed description of incentives structures offered to SEZ and non-SEZ area, respectively.

Furthermore, different incentive slabs were applicable to domestic and foreign investors with a special attention to foreign investors.[10] For example, the corporate income tax rate for these enclaves was 15 per cent, which was much lower than what was levied on domestic enterprises, that is 30 per cent. In addition, these enterprises were exempted from local income tax levied at the rate of 3 per cent. Foreign-funded manufacturing enterprises were given a two year exemption from corporate income tax and were permitted to pay income tax only at a half-tax rate for the subsequent two years. This was mainly meant to promote the fundamental objectives of SEZs, that is, to attract foreign investment rather than resorting to a reallocation of domestic resources from one region to another. However, after some time, SEZs witnessed illegal transfers of domestic capital to foreign countries which, in turn, returned to the country as repatriates' capital and invested in SEZs in the form of foreign investment in order to avail different types of incentives available to foreign investors (field observation). This, however, amounted to nothing more than shifting resources from one area to another rather than contributing towards the generation of an additional investment, leaving in its wake, a note of caution to be followed in offering various incentives towards the promotion of SEZs. Moreover, it also emphasized the need for proper checks and balances to be undertaken while allowing foreign investment in different sectors of the economy. For example, in the case of Shenzhen, foreign investment was concentrated on real estate development, leading to speculative activities in the initial years. As a result, the price of residential buildings rose at a very sharp rate.

In view of the initial success achieved in terms of attracting private and foreign capital towards boosting export performance and also technology transfer in the domestic market (initially restricted to these development zones), incentive structures were gradually extended to the rest of China with a view to promoting development in other priority sectors, specifically, the service sector, considering its low share in the gross domestic product (GDP) relative to the manufacturing sector. This reveals the dynamic policy strategies adopted by Chinese policymakers over the years to address the emerging challenges and development priorities. It is worth noting here that, despite

---

10 It seems quite surprising that China's policymakers had recognized the significance of FDI and its spillover benefits on the domestic economy way back in the 1980s, although this aspect got empirically validated and given due attention in the literature only in the recent past.

such a huge incentive structure made available to these enclaves, SEZs in China did not result in revenue loss to the government exchequer. This could be specifically attributed to a judicious geographical choice made in allocating and promoting SEZs in China (author's field observation). As explained elsewhere in the chapter, those regions opened up to such experiments were initially underdeveloped and had agriculture as the prime occupation. Thus, when the SEZ policy was introduced, it did contribute as expected towards government revenues rather than resulting in adverse fiscal situations.

Infrastructure as a tool to address supply side constraints

In addition to incentives packages, the significance of planning and infrastructure development was aptly recognized with special attention given to the promotion of SEZs (Yeh, 1985). For instance, in Shenzhen, a two-tier planning process was put in place (ibid). First, a Shenzhen Social and Economic Development Plan was formulated to deal with different issues related to population, migration and related issues. Second, a Master Plan was formulated for each of the zones to address issues related to land use and physical infrastructure. These were quite essential in the case of Chinese SEZs because, unlike EPZs in other countries, regions where Chinese SEZs were set up comprised real population. Thus, clearly, there was a need for careful planning and implementation of infrastructure policy required for the growth of industrial establishments and human settlement. In the whole process of promoting infrastructure, and thereby attracting foreign investors to SEZs, the Chinese followed the proverb 'Build a nest first; birds will follow later'.[11] Thus, they not only ensured a better industrial and urban infrastructure base, but also undertook proactive steps in this direction.

The Chinese policymakers did not stop with spelling out the need for promoting infrastructure facilities in each zone; rather, they followed it up with directing their attention towards zone-wise designation of responsibility for each of the tasks involved in building infrastructure. Under Article 5 of the Rules, respective municipal governments were vested with the legislative powers for taking appropriate steps towards building infrastructure facilities at the zonal level. For instance, the Guangdong Provincial Committee was charged with the responsibility of developing infrastructure facilities in the

---

11 As explained elsewhere in the chapter, it was a systematic approach followed in the promotion of various sectors that helped plan, to a large extent, the infrastructure requirement of these enclaves.

Guangdong region. Besides, wherever necessary, foreign-origin companies were allowed to participate in developing the infrastructure facilities. A distinct feature of the Chinese SEZ policy was its well thought-out plan for mobilizing resources needed for the development and maintenance of infrastructure facilities within each zone. Local governments were encouraged to undertake infrastructure projects as long as they were able to mobilize resources for the same through various avenues (Hameed, 1996). Major sources of local revenue included revenue generated from taxes, profit from SOEs, loans from banks, domestic and foreign investment, and a minimal contribution by the central government in the form of grants. However, these sources of revenue varied across zones. In the case of Shenzhen, a major source of revenue was from land use rights,[12] whereas for Xiamen, it came from the Xiamen municipal budget. Domestic and foreign investments were the major source of revenue for infrastructure development in the case of Hainan (Ibid.). In addition, private investment was largely encouraged. For instance, between 1980 and 1990, the central and local governments, accounted for 1.4 and 13.1 per cent of the total investments respectively in the physical infrastructure development of Shenzhen whereas the rest was channelized through private investments (Yeung *et al.*, 2009).

Shift in approach towards factors of production

In Communist China, historically, the government exercises absolute control over land and labour (Wall, 1993). This is because, the ownership of land rests with the government, and it decides on the land use pattern in the country. In addition, the presence of a strong Hukou system,[13] determined the scale of migration and supply of labour in urban areas, thereby strengthening the government's sway over land and labour. Thus, as part of economic reforms through SEZs, initiatives were taken to address the rigidities associated with land

---

12 In China's case, terminologies used in relation to land acquisition are different from elsewhere. For instances, in the case of India, government/purchaser has to pay compensation to purchase land ownership whereas, in China, compensation has to be paid to acquire 'right to use'. This is so because the system of private property and related concepts do not exist in China.

13 It is to be noted that, in the traditional Chinese economic system, migration between provinces was not allowed due to the rigid 'Hukou System', which categorized the population into temporary and permanent residents. Permanent residents were not only entitled to jobs but also got the benefits of various social security schemes provided by the local government. However, temporary residents were entitled to jobs on a temporary basis without any assurance of social security.

and labour markets.[14] Thus, apart from providing world class infrastructural facilities, the Chinese government also ensured an adequate supply of labour force for the operation of SEZs. For this purpose, a 'Labour Service Company' was set up in each zone, in accordance with Article 19 of Rule on SEZs, to meet the demands of foreign origin companies for professional employees. The above company was used mainly as an instrument for overcoming the barriers that existed in the labour market because of the Hukou system. This company supplied labour in different ways and channels (Chen, 1988). Initially, it was done via 'Transfer through Consultation and Selection', under which a team of officials from the concerned municipal organization would travel to different parts of the country for recruiting suitable candidates for the SEZs. In 1982, 'Recruitment through Examination and Invitation' came into operation under which, the concerned municipal government would advertise the posts to be filled up and selections were carried out accordingly. Under this system, an assurance was given to employees of housing facilities in the respective zones, and, often, employment for one's spouse was also provided for. Other incentives introduced to attract skilled labourers from mainland China included medical insurance, and permanent residency to workers and their family members irrespective of their past affiliations to Hukou, that is, irrespective of whether they were permanent or temporary residents or they were from rural or urban areas (Chu, 1985). Among other provisions, permanent residence gained greater importance because in the traditional Chinese economic system migration between provinces was not allowed due to the rigid 'Hukou System'. The third system was known as 'Borrowing and Offering Joint Appointment'. Under this provision, firms in Shenzhen entered a contract with their counterparts in the interior areas for hiring professionals for a specified period of time. However, these professionals were provided with only temporary residence cards. These different recruitment mechanisms could be categorized under two broad heads: those workers recruited through the first two channels enjoyed a permanent residence status in their respective regions, whereas those recruited under the third channel were treated as temporary residents. According to one estimate, in 1982 alone, between 20,000 and 30,000

---

14 Changes in approach towards capital market can be noticed in the government emphasis on fiscal and non-fiscal incentive measures to attract domestic and foreign capital. These incentive mechanisms helped attract capital to these enclaves, as already explained in the earlier section.

temporary workers were brought into the Shenzhen SEZ (Oborne, 1986). In addition, the government also made efforts to train man power within the region. Accordingly, a university was founded in Shenzhen by the municipal government (ibid).

Apart from putting in place such mechanisms, the companies across all zones were given freedom to hire the required labour force either through state agencies or with the help of SEZ developers, after obtaining the necessary approval of the respective provincial committees. Nevertheless, in either case, it was mandatory to have a contract between employer and employees with respect to wage rates, types of wages, bonus and other incentives to be provided. It was also mandatory (under Article 22) to act appropriately to protect the interests of labourers besides ensuring better working conditions. Furthermore, the enterprises were allowed to appoint workers, initially for six months on a probation basis (author's field observation). During this period, workers could be removed without going through any formalities or compensation. Post the probation period, a formal contract would be signed between the employer and the employee, after which companies would not be allowed to dismiss a worker without giving adequate explanation and/or proof. While protecting various labour-specific interests, interests of enterprises were also given a due attention in the SEZ policy framework. One such condition was that the employees return the training cost to the employer in the event of his/her quitting the job before the end of the contract period. This provision was made in the initial stage to ensure that SEZs were not misused just as training centre.

In addition to this, SEZs also helped to relax the state control over various issues related to labour market (Wall, 1993); in fact, they facilitated in a way, the emergence of a contract labour system in China in that the practice of 'iron rice bowl[15]' was relaxed for the first time in China. As a result, enterprises were no longer required to shoulder lifelong responsibilities with regard to their workers; in its place, a system of contract labour was introduced for the first time. Second, 'freedom to market one's own labour' was also encouraged for the first time. Specifically, in the case of Shenzhen SEZ, university graduates were allowed to seek jobs on their own as against the practice of getting assigned to workplaces. Third, a system of 'market intervention in food supply' was introduced in place of the conventional practice of 'rationing'.

15 It is a term used to refer to an occupation with a guaranteed job security, as well as steady income and benefits.

This was found to be quite helpful in the long-run in terms of relaxing the restrictions on the movement of labour from one region to another. Four, a 'system of moonlighting' was encouraged under which, workers were allowed to take up a second job, while still holding on to their 'iron rice bowl'. The other relaxations included 'Home Purchase Scheme' for workers, and a gradual reduction in the heavy subsidy offered by the government on workers' housing (Wong, 1987). However, it is worth noting here that, the government did not introduce any changes in the wage structure. Thus, wages were allowed to be determined by the enterprises, not through any mutual negotiation/bargaining (Wall, 1993). Undoubtedly, these interventions were quite helpful in breaking the traditional barriers associated with migration as well as improving labour productivity and competitiveness.

With regard to land, through SEZ policy, the Chinese government introduced reforms in the land market in urban areas. The practice of government ownership of land and its discretionary power over the land use pattern offered little security to foreign investors, as far as land ownership and tenancy management were concerned. Therefore, to boost investors' confidence in these enclaves, guidelines called 'the provisional regulations on land control in Shenzhen SEZs' were formulated and enacted in 1981 (Yeh, 1985), which spelt out in detail the role of Shenzhen government with regard to planning, land management, development and rent for land use by foreign investors. The guidelines consisted of six major conditions (ibid). First, all proposals related to land use were to be submitted to the Shenzhen government. Personal negotiations of any kind with landowners (on land use) were not allowed without the prior consent of the government. Second, a lease system was allowed for the first time in China, the conditions of which, however, varied depending on the volume of investment and type of land use.[16] Furthermore, different slabs of land use fee were introduced depending on its use, location and purpose, with a lower rate being applicable to industrial activities. This was in line with the government's commitment to promoting industrialization in the region. However, concessional rates were allowed for investments on education, healthcare, technology and other related domains, subject to a revision once in every three years. Three, foreign investors were required to obtain a land use certificate from Shenzhen municipal government. Fourth, in order to avoid illegal land transactions, a

---

16 The land rent further differs across zones (Nishitateno, 1983).

strict system was put in place to oversee such transactions. Fifth, in order to ensure that a given plot was developed for the purpose allotted *per se*, a strict time-frame was imposed. Accordingly, land use certificates were cancelled if foreign investors failed to follow the procedures. In addition, the government also made land developers accountable to environmental pollution, in terms of bearing the costs towards pollution reduction. In accordance with the decision to promote industrial activities by way of attracting foreign investment and to experiment with the capitalist mode of development, large tracts of agricultural land were diverted to non-agricultural purposes. Needless to add that adequate monetary compensation was given to the land-owning community along with an assurance of employment in the upcoming SEZ projects. Moreover, the government also made efforts to train farmers so as to make them employable in the emerging industries. This also resulted in the displaced farmers reaping handsome economic advantages in the process.

The above policy analysis clearly indicates that the Chinese policymakers were not only enthusiastic about experimenting with capitalism within a rigid socialistic framework through SEZs, but also gave their due attention to various nitty-gritty's in its promotion.

Trajectories of SEZ expansion in China – an empirical investigation[17]

The growth trajectories of SEZ expansion in China are elaborated in terms of the opportunities and economic transformation facilitated through SEZs followed by a discussion highlighting the challenges and economic set backs as inevitable side effects in the promotion of SEZs.

Opportunities and economic transformation of SEZs

Gross domestic product and economic transformation

All over the world, the dramatic economic growth of China has been recognized in terms of GDP growth. Measuring the performance of Shenzhen SEZs with the same yardstick indicates that the GDP growth of Shenzhen has been more significant and even surpassing China's national average. A similar trend is observed in terms of GDP growth rates also. Furthermore, the per capita income in respect of Shenzhen has remained above the national average

---

17 Originally published in *China Report*, Vol. 49, No. 2 Copyright 2013 © Institute of Chinese Studies, New Delhi. All rights reserved. Reproduced with the permission of the copyright holders and the publishers, Sage Publications India Pvt. Ltd, New Delhi. However, substantial changes have been made in this section.

**Figure 3.1: A Compartive Picture of Per Capita Income of
China and Shenzhen**

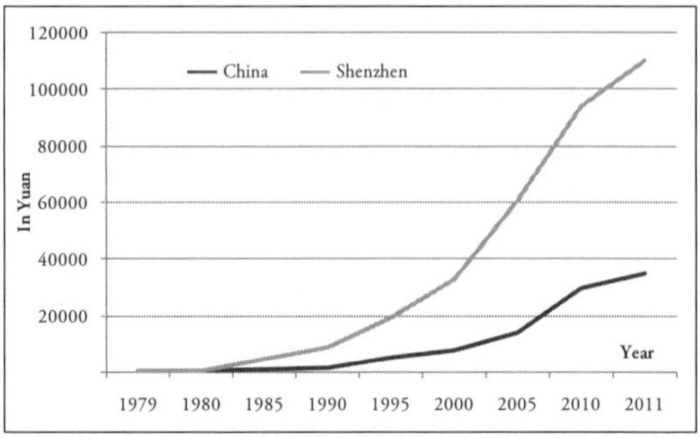

Source: CSY, 2012 and SZSY, 2013.

throughout the reforms period. In absolute terms, it is three times greater than the national average in 2011, thereby clearly indicating the economic strength of Shenzhen city (see Figure 3.1). Shenzhen's share in China's GDP shows a continuous increase over the years, the growth has been relatively very low – accounting for less than 3 per cent.

However, an analysis of the sectoral composition, Shenzhen's GDP *vis-à-vis* China since 1979, presents a few interesting facts (Table 3.2). First, the primary sector's share in GDP has been declining drastically. In particular, the decline has been more pronounced and faster in the case of Shenzhen, that is, from 37 per cent in 1979 to 0.1 per cent by 2010, whereas the national average shows a decline from 27.9 to 10.1 per cent over the same period and the share of the primary sector in GDP shows a rapid decline after 1980. Second, over the reference period the contribution of the secondary sector to GDP is observed to have remained almost constant for China as a whole showing significant improvement in the case of Shenzhen from 20.5 to 44.3 per cent, an increase by almost 2.5 times. Within the secondary sector, the share of the industrial sector in Shenzhen shows an improvement from 11.8 to 50.2 per cent, whereas the contribution of the construction sector has dropped from 8.7 to 3 per cent over the same period. Furthermore, within the industrial sector, the contribution of the light industry is found to be highly significant, accounting for almost 75 per cent of the total industrial output of Shenzhen SEZ in the early 1980s (Ge, 1999). Third, the tertiary sector in China has recorded an impressive growth in terms of its contribution to GDP from 24.2 per cent in 1979 to 43.2 per cent in 2010. However, the service sector in Shenzhen has made an impressive contribution to GDP from 1979 onwards from 42.5 to 55.6 per cent over the reference period.

Table 3.2: A Comparative Picture of GDP Composition by Sector: China and Shenzhen City

(In per cent)

Sectors	1978		1980		1985		1990		1995		2000		2005		2010	
	C	S*	C	S	C	S	C	S	C	S	C	S	C	S	C	S
Primary	27.9	37	29.9	28.9	28.2	6.7	26.9	4.1	19.8	1.5	14.8	0.7	12.6	0.2	10.1	0.1
Secondary	47.9	20.5	48.2	26	42.9	41.9	41.3	44.8	41.2	50.1	45.9	49.7	47.5	53.2	46.7	47.9
Tertiary	24.2	42.5	21.9	45.1	28.9	51.4	31.8	51.1	33	48.4	39.3	49.6	39.9	46.6	43.2	40.9

Source: CSY, 2012 and SZSY, 2013.
Note: C refers to China and S to Shenzhen; * data for Shenzhen relates to 1979.

The different patterns of growth noticed in the composition of Shenzhen GDP, specifically with respect to the secondary sector, could be traced to the approach designed for promotion of the manufacturing base in Shenzhen. Instead of becoming too ambitious about the SEZ policy, the process of industrialization in Shenzhen was introduced gradually in three stages (Wong and Chu, 1985). Initially, considering the inherent advantages and difficulties associated with the region, an emphasis was placed on the development of small-scale industries, especially labour-intensive but modern in nature. In the second stage, special emphasis was placed on high-technology industries. In the third stage, the industrial base of the region was diversified, specifically through the promotion of advanced technology-based industries with modern scientific methods of production. The approach as such was effective in ensuring additional employment generation in the economy besides developing the required infrastructure base in the region in a systematic manner without creating too much of a fiscal burden, in the process. However, this phenomenon of sectoral composition and its transition over the years seems to challenge the traditional process of 'development' as in the initial stage of economic development, the primary sector would have a significant share in the national income with the manufacturing sector followed by the service sector dominating the economic process in the subsequent period in terms of contributing to the national income. However, this does not seem to be the case in respect of Shenzhen's economy.

Participation in foreign trade and foreign investment

Prior to reforms, apart from the dominance of the central government with regard to planning and administration, the state enterprises dominated the industrial sector with a complete control over production, import and export of goods. There was hardly any scope for competition either from private or foreign origin companies which in turn, eventually affected the efficiency resource allocation and utilization and thereby the pace of economic growth and the composition of China's foreign trade. For example, China exported commodities in respect of which it had no comparative advantages nor producers enjoyed incentives of any kind to expand production, given a highly-centralized economic system. Furthermore, despite the availability of an abundant labour force, the production of capital-intensive products was encouraged (Lardy, 2007). Consequently, China's share in the world trade went down drastically from 1.5 per cent in 1953 to 0.6 per cent in 1977 (Lardy, 1994, 2007). It was in this context that the SEZ policy was designed to boost the export of labour-intensive products.

Although Shenzhen, started with low volume of foreign trade owing to the not so helpful economic conditions of the region, it managed to record surplus in its current account as against the national trend prevailing then. Within a few years, the performance of the Shenzhen SEZ showed an impressive improvement (Table 3.3) in that the value of its exports increased from US$ 900 million in 1978–79 to US$ 271,361 million by 2012. This outstanding performance related to trade promotion is reflected not only in the increase in absolute volume of trade, but also its increasing participation in the overall growth of national trade and its composition. By the end of 2010, Shenzhen's contribution to national trade constituted almost 12 per cent (Table 3.4). However, it is to be noted here that although the contribution of Shenzhen in China's GDP is relatively insignificant, it accounts for a major share in the country's aggregate trade volume.

Table 3.3: Trade Performance of China and Shenzhen over Time

(100 US million $)

Year	Export		Import		Total trade		Net trade balance	
	China	Shenzhen	China	Shenzhen	China	Shenzhen	China	Shenzhen
1978	97.5	0.09	108.9	0.07	206.4	0.16	-11.4	0.02
1980	181.2	0.11	200.2	0.06	381.4	0.17	-19.0	0.05

1985	273.5	5.63	422.5	7.24	696.0	12.87	-149.0	-1.61
1990	620.9	81.52	533.5	75.5	1154.4	157.02	87.4	6.02
1995	1487.8	205.27	1320.8	182.42	2808.6	387.69	167.0	22.85
2000	2492.0	345.63	2250.9	293.76	4742.9	639.39	241.1	51.87
2005	7619.5	1015.18	6599.5	812.99	14219.1	1828.17	1020.0	202.19
2010	15777.5	2041.8	13962.4	1425.6	29740.0	3467.4	1815.1	616.1

Source: CSY, 2012 and SZSY, 2013.

Table 3.4: Share of Shenzhen in China's Total Trade

Year	As percentage of China's export	As percentage of China's import	As percentage China's total trade
1980	0.06	0.03	0.04
1985	2.06	1.71	1.85
1990	13.13	14.15	13.60
1995	13.80	13.81	13.80
2000	13.87	13.05	13.48
2005	13.32	12.32	12.86
2010	12.94	10.21	11.65

Source: Calculation based on SZSY, 2013 and CSY, 2012.

With regard to import intensity[18] of Shenzhen's export, it is found that, while in the initial few years, it was on a higher side (85 per cent in 1980), it declined substantially over the years – as for the latest available year (2012) to 27 per cent. The declining trend was specifically noticed in the post-1990s when there was a near stagnation in the share of SEZs share to the country's aggregate exports. This high import intensity in the initial few years was influenced by the sectoral composition of the industrial activities in Shenzhen as discussed above. Specifically, in the early years, greater attention was placed on the assembling and processing operations. Such economic operations, in

18 This, in the present context, is measured as a simple ratio of net exports to total exports.

turn, depend on the components and other production materials sent by the parent company abroad (Wu, 1999). This could be related to the nature of trade policies in most of the industrialized countries of that time, which generally encouraged the use of their own raw materials and intermediate goods (Wu, 1999). Thus, the volume of imports by SEZs, among others, is correlated to the sectoral composition of a zone. This in turn should depend on the priorities of the development of industrial structure of the region in order to offset imbalances, if any, due to high import intensity.

In addition to facilitating trade expansion and diversification, another prime objective of the SEZ policy in China was to attract foreign investment for supplementing domestic investment. An analysis of the performance of the Shenzhen SEZ within this framework indicates that, Shenzhen initially started with a very low volume of foreign capital (US$ 30 million). It was only after the mid-1980s that the volume of foreign capital inflow started increasing very sharply (Table 3.5), barring a decline between 1995 and 2000 which could be attributed to the East Asian financial crisis. With regard to its composition, it is noticed that FDI constituted a large part of the total inflow of foreign capital in Shenzhen. Table 3.6 shows the mode of foreign capital influx in Shenzhen. Initially, foreign companies preferred to enter the Chinese market through cooperative ventures. However, joint ventures gradually replaced solo foreign companies after the late 1980s. This behavioural pattern and approach of foreign investors (MNCs) towards the reform process in China seems to have been motivated by the intention to understand the local market and demand situation before deciding on investment.

Table 3.5: Foreign Capital Inflow and its Components in Shenzhen
(100 US$ million)

	1979	1980	1985	1990	1995	2000	2003
Foreign loan	0 (0)	0 (0)	1.95 (18.82)	0.11 (1.53)	1.33 (3.71)	4.37 (16.54)	5.56 (9.53)
FDI	0.18 (59.99)	2.4 (89.36)	7.93 (77.28)	6.79 (97.92)	34.63 (96.29)	17.38 (65.84)	48.47 (83.15)
Others	0.12 (40.01)	0.32 (11.63)	0.4 (3.90)	0.04 (0.55)	0 (00)	4.65 (17.16)	4.38 (7.31)
Total	0.3	2.71	10.26	6.93	35.97	26.4	58.29

Source: SZSY, 2006.

Note: Figure in parentheses are percentage shares to the total; data not available for the recent years.

Table 3.6: Various Components of FDI Inflow in Shenzhen

	1979	1980	1985	1990	1995	2000	2003
FDI#	0.18	2.4	7.93	6.79	34.63	17.38	48.47
Joint Venture*	47.54	4.26	23.38	27.79	36.27	16.32	25.75
Cooperative operation*	52.46	58.27	73.18	23.71	18.35	6.86	2.3
Solo foreign companies*	0	37.47	3.45	48.5	45.38	74.07	69.23

Source: SZSY, 2006.
Note: * Values are in per cent; # values are in US$100 million; data not available for the recent years.

Table 3.7: Country of FDI Origin in Shenzhen

(In per cent)

Year	Hong Kong and Macau	Taiwan	Singapore	USA	Japan	France	Others
1986	46.64	0.00	9.76	2.04	17.11	6.55	17.89
1990	78.92	6.33	4.52	1.81	1.53	0.01	6.88
1995	76.41	2.04	2.21	4.73	5.82	1.08	7.71
2000	53.51	1.51	2.03	4.40	0.64	10.11	27.81
2003	58.38	3.14	1.70	2.93	1.72	0.64	31.49

Source: SZSY, 2006; data not available for the recent years.

With regard to the sectoral composition of FDI, it is found that in the early years of reform, the industrial sector in Shenzhen attracted a large share of FDI (Figure 3.2). Among other things, this could be due to the competitiveness of SEZs in the international market followed by the incentive structure available for the same (Ge, 1999) and the pattern of growth designed in the promotion of SEZs. Against this, the share of the agricultural sector in the total FDI inflow decreased from 3.6 per cent at the time of reform to almost zero by the end of 2005. Interestingly, two major shifts in the FDI inflow were noticed in the post-1990s. First, the share of 'other' sectors gradually improved from 15.6 per cent in the 1990s to 35.5 per cent in 2005. This was due to changes in China's foreign trade policy regarding new technology and research- and service-oriented foreign investment rather than manufacturing activities. Second, the real estate sector attracted a relatively higher share of foreign investment in the initial period due to a boom in the real estate markets of Hong Kong (Oborne, 1986). However, a sharp decline has been observed in the post-1990s due to various regulations imposed by the Shenzhen municipal administration division for avoiding undesirable consequences (author's field observations).

Figure 3.2: Sectoral Distribution of FDI in Shenzhen

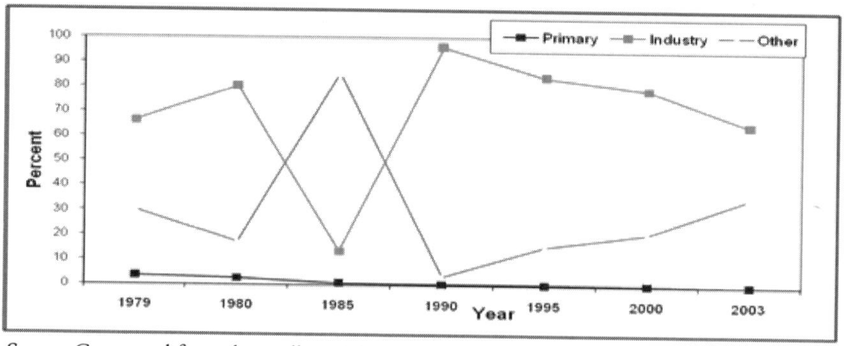

Source: Computed from data collected from CSY, 2006 and SZSY, 2006.
Note: Data not available for the recent years.

The direction of FDI inflow, however, shows that (Table 3.7) the SEZ policy was quite successful in meeting its agenda of attracting overseas investors from neighbouring Hong Kong, Macau and Taiwan. In fact, for the reference period of the study, the share of Hong Kong, Macau and Taiwan in FDI shows an increase from 46.64 to 61.52 per cent. However, this higher level of investment from Hong Kong has had an adverse impact on learning and adopting a better technology transfer in Shenzhen in view of a few Hong Kong firms using less complicated versions of their technology in their joint ventures in Shenzhen (Wu, 1999). Gradually though, Singapore, Japan, USA and France emerged as other FDI source countries with the shares of these 'other' countries increasing sharply from 17.89 per cent in 1979 to 31.49 per cent in 2005, indicating a diversification of foreign investment sources with regard to Shenzhen.

Employment and wage rate

Along with a higher GDP growth rate and a higher inflow of foreign investment, Shenzhen has been quite successful on the employment front as well. Over the years, employment opportunities in SEZs have increased substantially. However, due to the non-availability of data on employment indicators, here we have considered trends in the working population for analysing the employment scenario in the region. The figures presented in Table 3.8 shows a declining trend in the initial years (from 44 per cent in 1979 to 37 per cent in 1985), whereas significant improvement later (73 per cent in 2012). The initial decline could have been due to the conversion of agricultural land to non-agricultural purposes and also the fact that the rate of fall in employment generation in the agriculture sector could not have been compensated for by employment opportunities in the secondary and tertiary sectors. However, the increase recorded later could be ascribed to an upward swing in the inflow of foreign investments in Shenzhen (Ge, 1999) followed by an upsurge in the industrial activities in the region.

Table 3.8: Share of Working Population in Shenzhen (1979 to 2012)

(In per cent)

	1979	1980	1985	1990	1995	2000	2005	2010	2012
Working population	44.41	44.73	36.99	65.10	66.46	67.73	69.62	73.07	73.11

Source: Estimation based on SZSY, 2013.

The share of different sectors in generating employment, however, indicates that, the workforce in the agricultural sector had reduced drastically from 26 per cent in 1979 to 1 per cent by the end of 1997. At the same time, the industrial sector (45 per cent) followed by construction (10 per cent), commerce and restaurants (11 per cent) that emerged as promising sectors for generating employment (Park, 1997). The share of urban self-employment in the total employment increased from 2.94 per cent in 1979 to 55.84 per cent in 2012 (Table 3.9). This suggests a declining tendency of risk aversion among the Chinese because, by definition, this sector does not assure the type of social and working security that is available to workers in the SOEs, foreign and joint ventures. It is also found that the rate of employment generation in the Shenzhen SEZ declined after reaching the peak, particularly in the 1990s.

Table 3.9: Composition of Employment in Shenzhen

Year	Total employed#	Staff and workers (%)	Urban self employed (%)	Labourers of towns and villages (%)
1979	13.95	28.82	2.94	68.24
1980	14.89	32.64	2.55	64.81
1985	32.61	69.49	1.96	28.55
1990	109.22	50.73	3.08	46.19
1995	298.51	29.73	24.18	46.09
2000	474.97	19.66	29.45	50.89
2005	576.26	28.70	36.59	34.71
2010	758.14	33.11	49.67	16.95
2012	771.20	36.03	55.84	7.84

Source: SZSY, 2013.

Note: #indicates values are in 10,000 persons.

In the intervening time, wage rates also exhibited an upward swing. However, a comparison of the wage rates of staff and workers with those of SOEs indicates a steady increase in the wage rates of SOEs. This is in contrast to the general impression about SEZs as well as the empirical findings of earlier studies that wages in foreign-owned enterprises in Shenzhen were, on an average, higher than wages paid elsewhere in Shenzhen. This aspect got a further confirmation during personal interviews carried out in Shenzhen. This discrepancy raises doubts regarding the accuracy of statistics as presented by the Chinese government besides being challenged by other studies like those of the World Bank (1983).[19]

All the same, SEZs seem to have successfully met the various objectives underlying their promotion. However, as argued by Sen and Dreeze (1999), 'In learning from China, it is not enough to look only at positive lessons-what can be fruitfully emulated; it is important to examine the 'non-lessons' as well-what may be best avoided'. Thus, it is equally important to elaborate on the challenges and economic set backs of SEZ expansion in China.

---

19 The World Bank through an independent study estimated the real per capita GNP of China was much lower than what was claimed by China's official statistics.

Challenges and economic set backs in the context of SEZ expansion in China

The state of the agricultural sector in the SEZ period

One of the most obvious and inevitable fallouts results of SEZ promotion in China concerns a significant drop in the contribution of the primary sector including agriculture to Shenzhen GDP over the years (Figure 3.3). A comparison with the national trend reveals decline being much steeper in the case of Shenzhen than China. On the surface, it seems to be a welcome trend from the perspective of conventional stages of development. However, a closer scrutiny from a different perspective can help understand the scenario much better.

Figure 3.3: Share of Primary Sector to GDP of China and Shenzhen

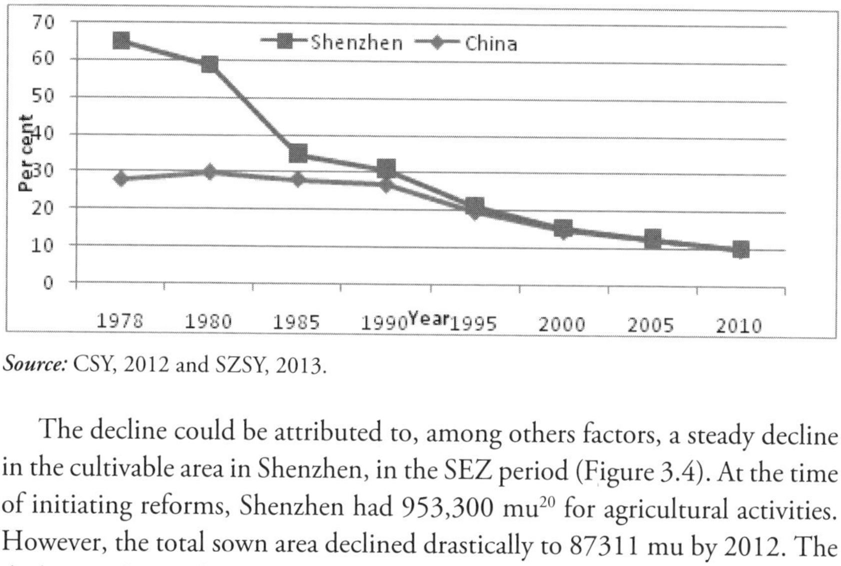

Source: CSY, 2012 and SZSY, 2013.

The decline could be attributed to, among others factors, a steady decline in the cultivable area in Shenzhen, in the SEZ period (Figure 3.4). At the time of initiating reforms, Shenzhen had 953,300 mu[20] for agricultural activities. However, the total sown area declined drastically to 87311 mu by 2012. The decline is observed particularly in respect of the area under food grain crops, that is, from 7,58,100 to 12 mu (SZSY, 2013). On an average in the post-reforms period, the decline in area available for agriculture was more than 90 per cent, which could be attributed to two major factors. One, a shift in the land use from agricultural to non-agricultural activities (Peimin, 2007); and second, a shift in terms of farmers and agricultural labourers turning to non-farming activities because of higher wages and better standards of

---

20 A *mu* is the Chinese method of measuring area under agriculture. It is equal to 0.0667 ha.

living (Zheng *et al.*, 1985). A similar compulsion could be behind a decline in the share of the primary sector at the national level, too. For instance, China lost, on an average, 14.5 million ha of cultivable land between 1979 and 1995 (Lichtenberg and Ding, 2008). Furthermore, between 1996 and 2005, more than 26 per cent of arable land was lost to non-agricultural uses in China (Goswami, 2007). This substantial reduction in the cultivable land at the national level is considered responsible for cultivable land loss in the coastal followed by central regions (Yang and Li, 2000). In this context, it should be noted that a majority of SEZs and ETDZs in China are located in the coastal region. In fact, the cultivable land loss in Guangdong and Fujian provinces (in which SEZs are located) is found much higher than the Chinese national average and is considered largely responsible for the steady expansion of land under non-agricultural uses (Yang and Li, 2000). To make matter worse, a large portion of land acquired initially from agriculture for industrial purpose has remained unutilized in China, specifically in development zones (Lichtenberg and Ding, 2008). For instance, more than 1 lakh ha of land in development zones currently remains unused, which no longer can be brought back to agricultural activities (Cai, 2003; Ho and Lin, 2004).

**Figure 3.4: Area under Cultivation in Shenzhen City:
A Post-SEZ Perspective**

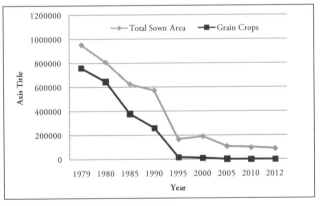

Source: Estimation based on SZSY, 2013.

This large-scale diversion of agricultural land towards urbanization and industrialization has had an adverse impact on food self-sufficiency of Shenzhen city in the recent years. For instance, in 1980–81, Shenzhen was not only self-sufficient in foodgrain production, but also was a regular supplier of 40 million catties to other parts of China (Zheng *et al.*, 1985). Today, it depends on other provinces for its day-to-day needs of grains and other basic food items. In this context, it is to be noted that the situation mirrors the problem an economy may face, if course corrections measures not taken with the problem intensifying and if such projects are promoted nationwide. The decrease in the cultivable land was more pronounced in the 1990s, corresponding to a decreased share of the agricultural sector in GDP. Moreover, over the same period, there was a decline in the cultivable area available per agricultural person and per agricultural labourer in Shenzhen, that is, 0.25 mu per agricultural person for 2000 (SZSY, 2006). Also visible was a drastic decline in the per capita cultivable land (Chen, 2007). In fact, China's per capita cultivable land is much lower (0.10 ha) than the corresponding figures for USA (0.47 ha) and European Union (0.69 ha; Lichtenberg and Ding, 2008). This implicitly points to a growing pressure of population on the agricultural sector in the post-1990s in view of the government restrictions on the movement of labourers from rural to urban areas. Furthermore, as elaborated in the previous section, agriculture was hardly successful in attracting foreign investment and creating the associated spillover effects. Thus, the agricultural sector faced two specific problems: a substantial drop in the land available for agriculture and the total failure to attract foreign investments. A fall in the share of cultivable area, a fall in the share of agriculture in GDP and a fall in the share of people dependent on agriculture may appear as part of the development process and this seems the case for all countries that have improved their income levels, that is, today's developed countries.

However, one may also argue that land is not the only factor of production in agriculture and that a decrease in the cultivable land can be compensated for by increasing other inputs for increasing production. The problem here is that the above argument presupposes the availability of irrigation, research and development, and other intermediate inputs, etc., whereas the absence of supportive inputs automatically negates the contention. Moreover, any such argument can certainly be challenged citing the law of diminishing marginal returns in the agricultural sector, that is, an increase in production by increasing inputs is impossible beyond a certain level (see Cannon, 1892). Nevertheless, there has been, in the recent years, a growing concern over the steady decline in the land available for cultivation in China. Therefore, in this respect, two important laws – the Basic Farmland Protection Policy (1994) and the New Land Administration Law (1999) – enacted by the Chinese government, reaffirm its commitment to the preservation of farmlands. In 2001, a goal was also set to secure at least 1.28 million ha of cultivable land (based on author's interviews, 2007) with each province setting different standards to ensure the same. The Chinese government also brought in an appropriate legislation to ensure the right to use of land as also to settle rural disputes. As a logical follow-up, commencing July 2003, an approval for new development zones in China was put on hold (Chen, 2007). These steps are expected to arrest the trend of declining cultivable land to a large extent.

The regional dimension of growth and demographic challenges

A steady increase in Shenzhen's GDP, reveals a sign of an imbalance in the growth across districts. For instance, the contribution of districts covered under the SEZ scheme is relatively higher than the ones in the non-SEZ districts (Table 3.10). This raises questions about the appropriateness of the SEZ scheme besides warranting further studies on the issue. In fact, Jones *et al.* (2003) argue that cities/provinces that had promoted different typologies of development zones were given preferential policies like tax breaks, favourable conditions for loans, credit and subsidies, higher foreign exchange retention rates, better fiscal autonomy, and speedy financial and legal approvals relative to other parts of China. Such policies subsequently benefited these regions, specifically the coastal areas at the cost of inland regions. Furthermore, these policies positively affected growth by way of providing business-friendly environments and, indirectly, by encouraging FDI inflows into these cities (Jones *et al.*, 2003). This is because, regions with SEZs have always received more than their natural share of government resources at the cost of the development of other regions. Furthermore, Ota (2003) and Srinivas (2004) among others, also argue that the creation of SEZs and development zones worsened regional disparities in China not only between SEZs and non-SEZ areas but also between rural and urban areas. As a result, huge gaps were observed in terms of income, social, physical and institutional infrastructure between SEZ and non-SEZ areas. Coastal regions developed at a faster rate than interior regions. For instance, in a relative sense, the coastal population was two times wealthier than the interior population (Fujita and Hu, 2001). Furthermore, the coastal areas developed more rapidly than the western regions of China; about 90 per cent of China's total population living in absolute poverty belongs to the western region (Jones *et al.*, 2003). The regional differences in growth were also reflected in the consumption expenditure (Davis, 2000). Such economic disparities between the regions have resulted in social unrest in the SEZ regions (see next section).

Table 3.10: GDP Composition by Districts in Shenzhen (2012)

(In per cent)

	SEZ districts	Non-SEZ district
GDP	53.50	46.50

Source: SZSY, 2013.

Over the last three decades, Shenzhen SEZ has allowed some scope for a few more mal-adjustments. This is visible not only in the economic sphere, but also the changing demographic pattern. For 2006, Shenzhen city recorded a population of nearly 8 million as against 300,000 in 1979. On an average, the population of Shenzhen has increased at the rate of 13.4 per cent. The floating population increased phenomenally from 0.5 per cent in 1979 to 72.73 per cent by 2012 (Table 3.11). This highlights a huge 'in migration' pattern caused by the creation of the SEZ in the city. However, the number of women in the total population has declined slightly from 54 per cent to 47 per cent over the reference period.

Table 3.11: Demographic Characteristics of Shenzhen

	1979	1980	1985	1990	1995	2000	2005	2010	2012
Total population	314100	332900	881500	1677800	4491500	7012400	8277500	10372000	10547400
Population with temporary resident cards[#]	0.5	3.6	45.7	59.1	77.9	82.2	78	75	72
Female composition in the total population[#]	54	54	49	49	48	48	47	46	47

Source: SZSY, 2006 .

Note: # Values are in per cent.

The latter developments can be attributed to two factors. First, a higher migration rate of men to Shenzhen city due to huge investments in the basic infrastructure coupled with the government publicity of Shenzhen as a promising land (Chen, 1988). In addition, the growing employment opportunities in Shenzhen city could have been the primary factor behind migration. Second, this could also have been due to the inevitable side effect of 'one child policy', which resulted in higher foetus deaths in view of preference for sons rather than daughters (see Hull, 1990; Banister, 1992). Undoubtedly, this large volume of migrant population in Shenzhen provided the labour force needed for the industrial development of Shenzhen. At the same time, this growing population also imposed additional costs on the city in terms of providing basic infrastructure facilities (Chen, 1988, 74), social unrest, crime and human trafficking in the region (Goswami, 2007).

The rising price index

The increase in wages and non-availability of basic foodstuffs pushed up the general consumer price indices in the region (Table 3.12 and Figure 3.5), over the reference period of the study, by almost eight times. For the earlier years, the price rise was caused by an increase in the prices of food. However, after 2000, this was further aggravated by an increase in the price indices of services as well. In addition to this, during the intervening time, the price index of Shenzhen was more than the general price index of China as a whole. One estimate notes that within three years of reforms, the cost of living in Shenzhen rose by 66.6 per cent, affecting the standard of living of those not employed by foreign companies.

Table 3.12: General Consumer Price Indices of Shenzhen

Year	Base year*	Preceding year
1980	105	105
1985	167.2	122.5
1990	331.2	101.6
1995	584.1	112.4
2000	658.8	102.8
2005	675.7	101.6
2010	777.7	103.5
2012	842.7	102.8

Source: SZSY, 2006.

Note: Base year 1979 = 100.

Figure 3.5: Price Indices of Shenzhen and China

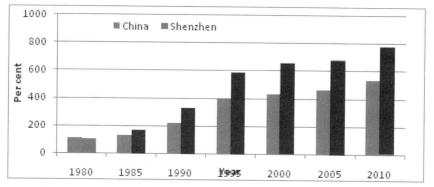

Source: Estimation based on SZSY, 2013 and CSY, 2012.

Summary

Undoubtedly, a larger part of SEZ success in China could be attributed to their systematic approach to defining and implementing the SEZ policy. It is not just the SEZ policy *per se*, which has enabled the transformation of a traditional economy into a modern one. Evidently, both internal and external factors have supported the government's commitment towards achieving the objectives of reforms through a prudent SEZ policy. Specifically, the break from the rigid economic system followed during the pre-reform period seems to have unlocked the latent potential of the economy, which, coupled with the subsequent reform measures, constitutes the main thrust for the success of reforms in China. Furthermore, initiatives undertaken at different levels of governance along with a decentralization process have contributed significantly to a higher level of efficiency in the management of SEZs. Moreover, it is to be noted that when China set up its SEZs, the international scenario was totally different as there was no WTO and its regulations, there were no restrictions on the use of incentives and subsidies as a tool to attract FDI. However, the conditions are completely different now which by themselves pose a different set of challenges to the process of trade liberalization.[21]

---

21 For instance, in the recent literature, it has been argued that most of the fiscal incentives and exemption in labour laws given to SEZs units do not follow the framework provided by these international organizations. A set of studies (Cling and Letilly, 2001; Madani, 1999; Jayanthakumaran, 2002) has illustrated that the Agreement on Subsidies and Countervailing Measures (ASCM), signed in 1994, as part of WTO, imposes new constraints, particularly on those countries with per capita income more than US$ 1,000. However, without making any special reference to SEZs, fiscal measures were

Apart from internal factors, a few external factors such as a strong and active presence of overseas Chinese investors have played a significant role in the success of reform measures. Furthermore, when China initiated the reform process, it hardly had any competitors in the world market, particularly in East Asia. Therefore, the timing of reform enabled them to reap the maximum possible. The Chinese way of handling the SEZ policy clearly demonstrates that incentives cannot be the sole facilitator in the promotion and success of SEZs and that there is a need to give proper attention to the development of a strong infrastructural base and the creation of an efficient administrative machinery. China's experiment with SEZ policy also indicates that the success or failure of economic reforms largely depends on whether or not reform measures identify and subsequently address the shortcomings that generally characterize the pre-reform economic conditions. The failure to understand the range of factors that have contributed to the successful implementation of the SEZ policy in China may lead to difficulties in identifying the pre-requisite conditions and supportive mechanism that need to be put in place for the efficient working of a policy. In this context, it is extremely important that a fair degree of caution is exercised in following another country's model of reforms especially while designing a policy towards imitating reforms in a developing country like India.

A performance analysis of Shenzhen SEZ, however, clearly demonstrates the role of SEZs in China's integration with the world economy. At the same time, it convincingly reinforces the contention that Chinese SEZs are not as green as hypothesized and claimed by Indian policymakers. In fact, the promotion of SEZs has resulted in a number of much maladjustment in the Chinese economy, not empirically explained by any of the studies. Importantly, it has special significance for countries like India, where the government has been trying to adopt and promote SEZs on an extensive scale. Thus, it calls for changes in the Indian context because; it would be difficult to reverse the process later on, even if so desired, because, unlike China, SEZs in India are not few in number. This indicates at the potential problems that may crop up in future, if preventive measures are not taken now.

---

prohibited from 2004. However, this ban applies only to the manufacturing industry, not agricultural products and service sector. Thus, it highlights the need for modifying exemptions given to these units within the framework under ASCM.

Annexure

Annexure Table 3.1: Incentive Structure for SEZs and Non-SEZ Areas in China

1. Income tax			
1.1.	Direct sale	SEZ	There is no local surtax. Passive China-source incomes like interest, royalties and license fees are subject to a 20 per cent withholding tax. However, this rate can be lowered from 10 to 0 per cent for contracts involving advanced technology, technical data and technical training.
1.2.	Equity joint venture	Non-SEZs	The rate of taxation on net income is set at 30 per cent along with 3 per cent local surtax. However, companies may apply for exemption for the first two profit making years and a 50 per cent reduction for the following three years.
		SEZs	Income tax rate is at 15 per cent without any local surtax. Ventures commencing operations before 1985, or investing more than HK$ 5 million using advanced technology, those having a long lead time, or considered as highly desirable, may apply for exemption for the first three profit-making years or a reduction of 20–50 per cent (in Shenzhen); this exemption can be extended up to five years (Xiamen). Investors whose profits are reinvested for no less than five years can apply for tax reduction/exemption on reinvested profits.
1.3.	Wholly foreign owned enterprises	Non-SEZs	They require special authorization to start business outside SEZs.
		SEZs	They are allowed to settle in SEZs and ETDZs. They enjoy similar treatment as do joint ventures.
1.4.	Accelerated deprecation	Non SEZs	Straight line method is usually used. Depreciation period is between five years for electronic equipments and 30 years for buildings
		SEZs	Faster depreciation rates can be granted to joint ventures inside the SEZs.

1.5.	Remittance tax	Non-SEZs	After all taxes and legal transaction funds are paid. The same treatment applies for capital remitted abroad after a 10 per cent withholding tax is paid. The same applies for capital remitted abroad after the termination/liquidation of a company, once all liabilities and taxes have been paid.
		SEZs	No withholding tax
1.6.	Import tax	Non-SEZs	Not clear
		SEZs	Investment goods and raw material are exempted. Consumer goods can enjoy a reduction/exemption of import tax.
1.7.	Export tax	Non-SEZs	
		SEZs	No export tax levied on goods exported or delivered within the SEZs. However, goods delivered to domestic market are subject to export tax, and to the repayment of import taxes not levied on the inputs incorporated.
1.8.	Commercial and Industrial Consolidated Tax (CICT)	Non-SEZs	Capital contributed in the form of imported machinery equipment and spare parts, or additional capital of the same sort can be exempt from CICT, provided imported items are produced in China. Enterprises experiencing difficulties in paying CICT for sales on the domestic market can apply for reduction/exemption. Enterprises may apply for exemption on CICT for export goods, except for a few commodities.

		SEZs	Exemption from CICT based on approval as available for the following: • construction or production imports; • reasonable amount of office supplies; • means of transportation imported by foreign representatives for their own use; and • food and beverages imported for tourists and restaurants can be exempt from CICT upon approval. A 50 per cent reduction of CICT available on imported high tax commodities. If goods are manufactured mainly for export purposes, no CICT is levied at the factory level, except for a few. In Shenzhen, municipal authorities consider lowering the rate of CICT when applicable.
1.9.	Local taxes[22]	Non-SEZs	They are assessed at the discretion of local authorities
		SEZs	No local surtax levied on net income.
1.10	Personal taxes	Non-SEZs	Foreign personnel staying less than five years on their word, and with no intentions of becoming residents, irrespective of whether or not they remit their overseas income to China, are not required to report or pay tax on their oversees profit.
		SEZs	Income earned inside China will enjoy a 50 per cent tax cut. After tax, income can be freely remitted without paying any withholding tax. In addition to this, foreign employees enjoy reduction/exemption of import tax on daily life necessities.

22 Local taxes include net income surtax, real estate tax, vehicle license tax, vessels and license tax.

1.11	Special conditions for ethnic Chinese investors	Non-SEZs	No special consideration
		SEZs	In Xiamen, Taiwan investors who wish to invest in the SEZ will enjoy a special preferential treatment in respect to income tax. There will be no income tax levied on foreign workers in any overseas Chinese investment.

2. Costs

2.1.	Industrial land rents	SEZ	Industrial land rent in Shenzhen is in the range HK$ 19–32 per m²/year; in Shantou HK$ 16–64 per m²/year. In the three Guangdong zones, this rent can be revalued every three year by a rate not exceeding 30 per cent. In Xiamen, rent is in the range HK$ 3–63 per m²/year and can be revalued every five years by less than 20 per cent.
2.2.	Industrial standardized buildings	SEZ	The SEZ development companies provide standardized office spaces for investors. In Shenzhen, the monthly range is HK$ 1,200 per m².
2.3.	Purchase of workshop	SEZ	A company which so wishes can purchase workshops. In Shenzhen the rate is HK$ 1,100–1,900 per m²; in Shantou it is HK$ 1,200 m².
2.4.	Water and energy	SEZ	These costs are said to be lower than in Hong Kong; water 0.18 Rmb/m³; electricity: 0.085 Rmb/KWh for industrial use; 0.2 Rmb/KWh for domestic use.
2.5.	Participation in infrastructure cost	SEZ	If a company is located in a place where there is no infrastructure, then the respective company is required to pay a specified amount for construction fees.

2.6.	Labour costs	SEZ	Labour cost has three components (1984): 70 per cent is given directly to labour; 25 per cent is used for social labour insurance and to companies for various state subsidies for workers and 5 per cent is reserved by the enterprises to subsidize their welfare funds.
			Labour costs vary from about HK$ 500 in Shantou, Zuhai and Xiamen to around HK$ 700 in Shenzhen and HK$ 800 in Shakou.
			Wages are to be increased each year between 5 per cent and 15 per cent. An amount equivalent to 2 per cent of the total wage bill must be given to labour trade unions.
			Enterprises are allowed to choose the system of remuneration,[23] work schedule.
2.7.	Currency and settlements	SEZ	Usually, foreign currencies are used to pay costs described above. But if Rmb is earned through access to the domestic market, companies may apply for using them to settle these costs.
2.8.	Rate of change	SEZ	Net hard currency earnings from exports are entitled to be changed into Rmb at international settlement rates (2.8 Rmb/$) rather than official rates (2.5 Rmb/$ in September 1984) by the Bank of China.
2.9.	Special consideration for ethnic Chinese investors	SEZ	In Xiamen, Taiwanese investors enjoy special conditions for land rent.

---

23 It includes piecework, hourly basis, daily basis, proposition of fixed and floating wages.

3. Relation with the domestic market			
3.1.	Access to domestic inputs	Non-SEZ	Material needed by a joint venture should be priced according to the current prices in China and paid in Rmb except for precious metals, petroleum, coal, and timber that are valued at their international prices and paid for in Rmb. However, material falling under the category of goods imported (or exported) by China, will be priced according to the c.i.f. international prices plus import duty and business tax import commission fees (respectively according to the international f.o.b. prices)
		SEZ	Companies within SEZ do not usually pay tax on imported goods from abroad; therefore, goods exported by China are priced preferentially on the basis of their international f.o.b. prices.
3.2.	Access to domestic market	Non-SEZ	On a case by case basis, a wider access to the domestic market can be granted to goods that are otherwise imported by China. Products should be sold to the relevant foreign trade cooperation at a value related to their international prices, and usually paid for in foreign currency.
		SEZ	Unlike projects in the 14 coastal cities or others in the rest of China that are often renovation projects, investments in the SEZs should be export oriented. The ratio of domestic sales (average 20 per cent) depends upon demand.
3.3.	Special condition for Chinese overseas	SEZ	In Xiamen, Taiwan investors are permitted to sell at least 30 per cent of their production on the domestic market. In addition to this, they enjoy preferential rates on the loans in Rmb or in foreign currency.

Source: Adopted from Oborne (1986).

4

Performance of Special Economic Zones: Promises, Realizations and Paradoxes

Background

Special economic zones in the Indian context are improved versions of export processing zones on the lines of China's SEZs. Compared to EPZs, the current SEZ policy is more concrete in terms of objectives as well as institutional arrangements. Thus, such a pragmatic shift in the policy regime towards better institutional arrangements and world class infrastructure has helped increase confidence of investors over time, as can be clearly observed from a steady increase in the number of SEZ projects that have been approved in the country and also in the steep increase in the number of exporting units within such enclaves. In this connection, it would be interesting to explore: (a) how have SEZs, with a more nuanced trade policy regime governing them, fared in comparison with EPZs? That is, whether the policy intervention in 2000 has had any positive impact on the working and performance of SEZs; and (b) what are the corresponding dimensions at the disaggregate level? In this context, earlier studies, while analysing the trade performance of Indian EPZs/SEZs, seem to have failed in analysing rigorously the effectiveness of SEZs over EPZs both at the aggregate and disaggregate levels. Rather what is presented in the literature seems mere description of the data available over the years. Furthermore, there is dearth of studies that look into whether there exist variations in the performance of SEZs across zones from a holistic perspective.

These issues are explored and analysed in this chapter based on the aggregated data collected from the seven conventional SEZs,[1] namely Kandla, Santacruz, Noida, Cochin, Chennai, Falta and Vizag. Needless to add here that the inclusion of new SEZs in the study will not help throw much light on the issue of SEZ-effectiveness over EPZs. Meanwhile, the primary findings and insights gained during author's extended first-hand fieldwork in these seven zones[2] have been utilized to validate the main findings. The analysis has been carried out for the period 1986–87 to 2007–08[3] with the time period under consideration being long enough to analyse the effectiveness of the SEZ policy, enacted in 2000–01, as against that of the EPZs. A brief account of each SEZ is provided in Table 4.1.

Trade performance of SEZs at the aggregate level[4]

The basic purpose underlying the SEZ policy has been to enhance the production of exportable commodities in an environment free of the usual constraints associated with the domestic industry. Therefore, trends in the EPZ/SEZ trade can be seen as a proxy for analysing the effectiveness of the policy. This section is an attempt in that direction. Time series data on SEZ exports and imports for the reference period presents two major breaks (Table 4.2). The first break in trend is noticeable for the early 1990s[5] owing to two

---

1   Since the focus of the study was to analyse the effectiveness of SEZs over the EPZs structure in India, in this context this is to be noted that all the seven selected SEZs represent the entire population of SEZs in the country as they were the only functional EPZs prior to the introduction of the SEZ policy in the country.

2   Carried out between December 2006 and January 2014.

3   Although the present analysis remains restricted to the period from 1986–87 to 2007–08, wherever necessary, we have provided scenarios as prevailing in the 1970s and 1980s.

4   Originally published in *Journal of Asian Public Policy*, Vol. 5, Issue 1: 23–40, www.tandfonline.com/http://www.tandfonline.com/doi/full/10.1080/17516234.2012.66 1948. However, substantial revisions have been made in this section.

5   Also, the early 1970s witnessed changes in the trend of SEZ exports. This break in the trend was consistent with India's exports. At this particular juncture, the country's exports (in value terms) more than doubled following the depreciation of the Indian currency. As Nayyar (1976) noted, there was a 21 per cent increase in the rupee value of India's exports in the first half of the 1970s.

In addition to this, the late 1980s also witnessed an improvement in the exports of these enclaves in view of number of zones operating in the country increasing from two to six.

Table 4.1: A Brief Profile of the Select Indian SEZs

SEZ	State	Sector	Year of establishment	Year of conversion to SEZ	Area#	Units*	Jurisdiction	Remarks
Kandla	Gujarat	Multi-product	1965	2000	1000	169	Gujarat	First FTZ
Santa Cruz	Maharashtra	Electronics and gems and jewellery	1975	2000	104	290	Maharashtra, Goa	First EPZ
Noida	Uttar Pradesh	Multi-product	1986	2003	310	162	UP, Rajasthan, Haryana, Uttaranchal, Punjab, Delhi, Chandigarh, HP, J&K	First EPZ without any ready availability of port and airport in the vicinity
Falta	West Bengal	Multi-product	1986	2003	280	128	All eastern and northeastern states	First zone with proximity to DC office
Chennai	Tamil Nadu	Multi-product	1986	2003	103	111	Tamil Nadu and Lakshadweep	--
Cochin	Kerala	Multi-product	1986	2000	103	82	Kerala, Karnataka and Lakshadweep	First plastic-free zone in the country
Vizag	Andhra Pradesh	Multi-product	1994	2003	360	43	Andhra Pradesh	Youngest among the seven conventional EPZs (centrally owned)

Source: Author's compilation.
Note: # indicates values in acres; * denotes actual numbers for 2007–08.

major policy developments. First, an improvement in the general economic scenario of the country, in the post-reform period, particularly in the form of, the reduced tariff rates, easing of quantitative restrictions on exports and imports and the measures undertaken to rationalize the exchange rate. The second relates to specific policy initiatives undertaken to carry out reforms in the EPZ framework with the most important among them being the permission given to DTA sale up to 25 per cent of production on payment of 50 per cent of custom duties and providing for the role of the state and private sector in the EPZ structure of the country. Thus, it supports the argument that though these zones are considered as exclusively separate economic entities for promoting export growth, the general macro-economic framework and the corresponding business climate of the country vastly influence the outcome of these zones along with specific policy initiatives undertaken to address issues concerning to SEZs. This in turn, also explains implicitly the factors responsible for the poor performance of EPZs up to 1990s. The second break is noticed for 2000–01, following the introduction of the SEZ policy in the country. Over a period of eight years, since the introduction of the SEZ policy in the country, the value of exports generated by the seven conventional SEZs increased by almost three-fold. Except for 2001–02, SEZ exports have shown a positive trend, but with a greater degree of volatility.

Table 4.2: Trade Scenario of EPZs/SEZs
(For select years, from 1986–87 to 2007–08)

Year	Total SEZ export		Total SEZ import		NFE	
	Value ₹ (Crore)	Growth rate	Value ₹ (Crore)	Growth rate	Value ₹ (Crore)	Growth rate
1986–87	975.96		624.39		351.57	
1990–91	1822.54	17.02	1181.62	13.13	640.92	24.93
1995–96	3896.51	14.91	2641.94	33.28	1254.56	-10.94
1999–00	6716.23	23.53	3032.00	37.29	3684.22	14.11
2000–01	10053.62	49.69	3583.34	18.18	6470.28	75.62
2001–02	8009.60	-20.33	4456.74	24.37	3552.86	-45.09

Year	Total SEZ export		Total SEZ import		NFE	
	Value ₹ (Crore)	Growth rate	Value ₹ (Crore)	Growth rate	Value ₹ (Crore)	Growth rate
2002–03	8323.65	3.92	5183.05	16.30	3140.61	-11.60
2003–04	9781.32	17.51	5968.61	15.16	3812.71	21.40
2004–05	12575.74	28.57	8983.27	50.51	3592.47	-5.78
2005–06	15428.38	22.68	9667.57	7.62	5760.82	60.36
2006–07	17508.71	13.48	11670.85	20.72	5837.86	1.34
2007–08	21195.77	21.06	15832.97	35.66	5362.80	-8.14
Trend Growth Rate (CAGR)						
1986–87 to 2007–08	16.90		18.30			

Source: Based on the data collected from the selected SEZ development commissioner offices.
Note: Growth rate is expressed as an annual per cent changes over the preceding year.

A setback in the value of exports and its growth rate noticed for 2001–02, among others, could be attributed to the switchover of couple of units from the EPZ framework to EOUs rather than accept SEZ scheme.[6] In the case of Vizag SEZ, for instance, soon after the announcement of the SEZ policy, units like Synergies (an exporting unit), which had been dominating the trade scenario during the EPZ phase, preferred to shift their economic base from EPZ centric activities to EOUs rather than getting into the SEZ regime. This has had a corresponding impact on the trade performance of Vizag SEZ.[7] On the eve of the withdrawal of Synergies, the export value of Vizag SEZ had fallen from ₹ 1956 crore in 2002–03 to ₹ 534 crore in 2003–04. Furthermore, between 2000 and 2003, a decline in the number of exporting units operating within most of the seven conventional SEZs

6 Since the former allows 50 per cent of the sale of production in the domestic market without any additional tax. However, such transaction under the SEZs scheme requires the payment of custom duties because the SEZs policy does not allow sale in the domestic market.

7 Vizag EPZ was brought under the SEZs framework in 2003 along with Noida, Falta and Chennai EPZs.

could be observed. For instance, in the case of Kandla and Santacruz SEZs, the number of exporting units dropped, respectively, from 129 to 109 and 150 to 103 between 1999–2000 and 2000–01,[8] though the same increased in the subsequent year. If one were to look at total SEZ exports for the year 2012–13, 173 SEZs together account for ₹ 47,615 crore worth of exports.

The contribution of EPZs/SEZs to the country's exports and imports, however (Figure 4.1), shows a positive increase over the years. During the 1970s, the contribution of SEZs in the total exports and imports of the country was, respectively, 0.02 and 0.03 per cent. In the last 25 years, the share of SEZs in the country's exports and imports has shown a gradual increase with a few major breaks in terms of trend. One can notice, between 1980–81 and 1985–86, the share of EPZs in the country's exports and imports picking up very sharply from 0.67 and 0.22 to 3.05 and 1.02, respectively. This sudden rise in the share of EPZs in India's trade could be attributed to the emergence of gems and jewellery sector in Santacruz EPZ. However, in the current SEZs period (after 2000), there has been a decrease observed in the contribution of SEZs to India's trade for two consecutive time-spans (from 2000–01 to 2002–03). As already explained, following the introduction of SEZ policy, a couple of units, which were willing to concentrate on the domestic market, switched their economic base from EPZs to EOUs rather than getting into the SEZ regime. While looking at the period from 2000–01 to 2007–08 (during which the EPZ policy was substantially liberalized with the implementation of the SEZ framework), one can observe an upward trend in the relative share of SEZs in the country's exports and imports after an initial two year fall in the same. However, the value of the exports of all functional SEZs in India for 2012–13 accounts for about 29.12 per cent of country's total exports, a highly appreciable development. This reveals the growing dependence of India's exports on SEZ exports. However, if we compare the contribution of such enclaves with other countries, it becomes oblivious that India's SEZs are way below in terms of performance. For example, Shenzhen SEZ[9] alone

---

8   Kandla, Santacruz, Cochin and Surat SEZs were brought under the SEZ purview in 2000.

9   In this context, it is to be noted that, China has six SEZs. Fourteen coastal regions opened up for foreign trade. In addition, 15 free trade zones, 32 state-level economic and technological development zones and 53 new and high-tech industrial development zones were established in large and medium-sized cities with a view to attract technology-intensive and export-oriented industries.

contributed over 12 per cent to China's total trade for the year 2010 (CSY, 2012; SZSY, 2013). This comparison is only to point out that there exists a vast scope for further improvement in the performance of SEZs in the Indian context, particularly in view of a rise in the number of such zones operating in the country.

Figure 4.1: The Share of EPZs/SEZs in the Country's Aggregate Exports and Imports

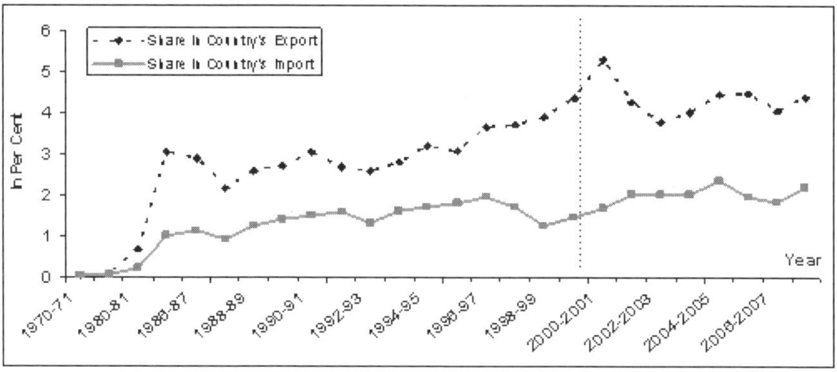

Source: Based on the data collected from the selected SEZ development commissioner offices and RBI Annual Report 2007–08.
Note: Values are in per cent.

The value of SEZ imports, however, displays more or less a similar pattern of growth for the reference period. However, it should be noted that, despite an increase in the gross value of exports, no substantial increase in the net foreign exchange earnings from these enclaves has been noticed. In fact, the net foreign exchange earnings from these enclaves for 2007–08 are found relatively less corresponding to 2000–01. This pattern among others could be attributed to a higher import intensity of SEZ exports (Figure 4.2), which, in turn, seems to have been guided by two factors. First, changes in the sectoral composition of exports towards highly capital-intensive and high-value products. Second, a rise in the number of exporting units during the SEZ period, generating a higher demand for imports at the implementation stage without leading to a corresponding increase in exports. Even in the context of other Asian EPZs/SEZs, a similar pattern of higher gross exports without getting reflected in the NFE earnings has been observed (see, for details, Amirahamdi and Wu, 1995).

Figure 4.2: Trend in Import Intensity of SEZs

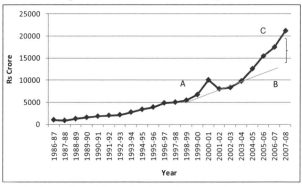

Source: Based on the data collected from the selected SEZ development commissioner offices.

Figure 4.3: Trend in SEZs Exports

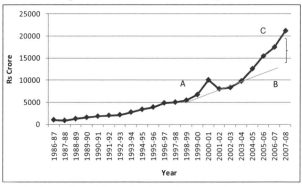

Source: Based on the data collected from the selected SEZ development commissioner offices.

Figure 4.4: Per Exporting Unit Productivity of EPZs/SEZs over the Years

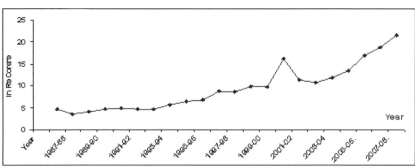

Source: Based on the data collected from the selected SEZ development commissioner offices.

Data presented in Table 4.2 and a graphical illustration (4.3) helps us infer a structural break for 2000–01 (Figure 4.1). In the absence of any policy changes, one could expect growth in the SEZs exports to the tune of AB, but in view of policy interventions SEZ exports grew AC over the years. A similar pattern has been observed in the case of exports generated by per exporting unit (Figure 4.4). To test the results statistically (obtained through a graphical representation), we employed a structural stability (dummy) regression model.[10] The functional form of the structural stability regression can be expressed as follows:

$$Y = \alpha_1 + \alpha_2 D_1 + \beta_1 t_t + \beta_2 (Dt) + u_t, \qquad (4.1)$$

where Y indicates exports; D is the dummy variable. It takes on the value 0 for EPZ period (1986–87 to 1999–2000) and 1 for the SEZs period (2001–01 to 2007–08); T is the time period.[11]

In this model, whether the introduction of SEZ policy in the place of its predecessors, namely EPZs, has any significant impact on the performance is explained based on the significance of the coefficients of the dummy intercept and slope coefficients. If both are statistically significant, then it implies that the SEZ policy intervention has had a statistically significant impact on performance. If dummy intercept reveals statistically insignificant value then null hypothesis of there is no impact of policy changes on the performance of SEZs tend to accept. Results presented in Table 4.3 clearly demonstrate a break in terms of trade performances since the intercept and slope dummy coefficients are found statistically significant at 1 per cent. This substantiates the strong impact of policy changes on the overall working of SEZs in the country. However, it should be noted that the coefficients of the dummy intercept though found statistically significant has revealed a negative sign. This needs to be interpreted very carefully. Since slope coefficient has revealed signs of significant and positive impact, the negative sign of dummy intercept does not imply that the introduction of the SEZ policy has a negative impact on performance. Rather, as outlined above this could be due to the fall in the number of exporting units and the corresponding fall in the exports between 2000–01 and 2001–02.

---

10 Chow test is not feasible in the present analysis due to limited number of observations, with a lesser degree of freedom.

11 In the model, β_1 and β_2 represent coefficients of the respective parameters.

Table 4.3: Results of Structural Stability Regression

Dependent variable: Exports
N: 22; K: 4; R^2: 0.94; Df:18

Coefficients	Coefficient value	t value
Constant	-210.71	-.297
Time	433.94	5.201*
Dummy	-19877.13	-5.388*
Time*dummy	1347.003	6.373*

Source: Author's estimation.

Note: * significant at 1 per cent level.

While comparing the trend in the growth rate (CAGR) of exports and imports between two time periods 1992–93 to 1999–2000 (pre-SEZ period/ EPZs period) and 2000–01 to 2007–08 (current SEZs period) – it is noted that the growth rate of SEZs imports has increased sharply from 10.83 to 23.21 per cent between the two time periods. Contrary to this, there was a decline in the growth rate of exports, from 16.00 to 14.56 per cent (Figure 4.5). Thus, an increase in the absolute value of exports during the current SEZ period in comparison with EPZ regime could not be substantiated with the trend growth rate for the same (CAGR). Moreover, on an average, SEZ imports have grown faster than SEZ exports. During the period between 1986–87 and 2007–08, the average growth rate of imports was 18.30 per cent, 1.40 percentage higher than that of SEZ exports (Table 4.2). Despite the overriding value of imports, the SEZs exhibited a positive trade balance during the period under analysis. The higher growth of imports over exports during the current SEZs period is due to the increase in the entry of new units under the SEZs regime. This is evident even in the CAGR of units, which is higher during current SEZ period compared to EPZ regime (Figure 4.6).

Figure 4.5: Compound Annual Growth Rate of EPZs and SEZs Trade

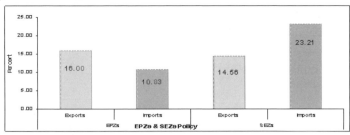

Source: Based on data collected from the seven conventional SEZ development commissioner offices.

Figure 4.6: CAGR of Exporting Units during EPZ and SEZ Regime

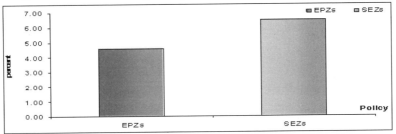

Source: Based on data collected from the seven conventional SEZs' development commissioner offices.

Structure of SEZ exports

Increase in exports value and its share in national trade, however, cannot be taken as the sole indicator to evaluate the current SEZ policy due to two reasons. First, the increase in value of SEZs exports may be due to substantial increase in world prices for goods and services. If so, it tends to indicate the possibility of a very little increase in the value of SEZ exports in real terms. Second, the substantial increase in value of exports from these enclaves could be due to realignment of investment[12] from domestic area to SEZs, as the latter provides bunch of fiscal and non-fiscal incentives to both SEZ exporters and developers. Given this, the effectiveness of the policy could be located in its capacity to diversify country's export basket as it reduces the threat of international volatility and associated export instability.[13] The effectiveness of SEZs in diversifying export basket, in particular, can be tested in two ways. First, through locating the sectoral distribution of newly approved SEZs in the country. This explains how much cautiously the government is in putting forward its agenda of promoting strong industrial policy (as a part of the industrial policy) and henceforth diversifying export basket (as a part of the trade policy). This can possibly be used as a proxy to capture whether there exists any divergence or convergence between industrial and trade policy of the country.[14] Second, the effectiveness of SEZs in diversifying country's

---

12 One such apprehension prevails within the government departments. For instance the Central Board for Direct Tax (CBDT) states that there is a considerable evidence to show that there has been a realignment of investment from domestic areas to SEZs.

13 For a debate on the possible correlation between export instability and export diversification, refer Masell (1970), Kingston (1973) and Kingston (1976).

14 Detail pertaining to sector-wise distribution of SEZ and related discussions are provided in chapter 2.

export basket could also be captured through analysing sectoral distribution of SEZ exports among the existing operational SEZs in the country.

This has been analysed through outlining the broad structure of SEZs export, followed by estimating a 'Hirschman Sectoral Concentration' Index, which is defined as the square root of the sum of the squared shares of export of each industry in total export from the country (in the present context SEZ) under study.

$$H = \sqrt{[\Sigma(X_i/X_t)^2]}, \tag{4.2}$$

where X_i is the individual sector export and X_t and total export of individual SEZs.

The value of H_C depends on two factors: (a) the number of products; and (b) the distribution of the shares of the products. In the literature, concentration and diversification index are used interchangeably. Higher the value, higher is the sectoral concentration; however, a lower value indicates increased diversification of export basket.

Figure 4.7: Structure of SEZs Exports, by Broad Sector Divisions
(1986–87 to 2007–08)

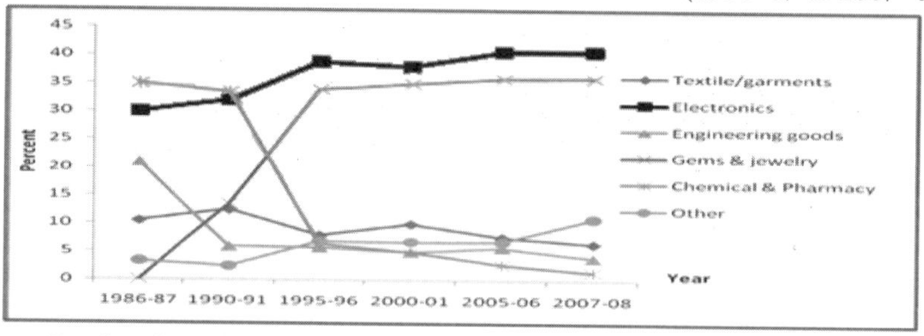

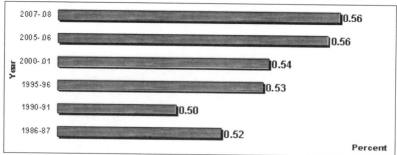

Source: Based on data collected from the seven conventional SEZs' development commissioner offices.

Figure 4.8: Trends in Sectoral Concentration Index of SEZs

Source: Based on data collected from the seven conventional SEZs' development commissioner offices.

Figure 4.9: Trends in Direction of EPZ/SEZ Exports

(1986–87 to 2007–08)

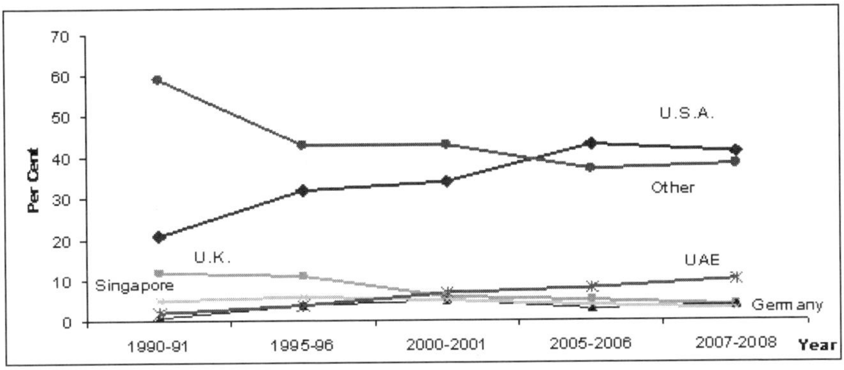

Source: Based on data collected from the seven conventional SEZs' development commissioner offices.

Sectoral distribution of seven conventional SEZs (Figure 4.7) clearly indicate that until the mid-80s, chemicals and pharmacy followed by electronics goods had the highest share in the total trade of the country. They accounted for almost 66 per cent of the total exports of SEZs for 1986–87. This is followed by engineering and textile garments. The early 1990s witnessed changes in the composition of exports largely due to emergence of gems and jewellery units in Santacruz EPZ in the late 1980s. Since then gems and jewellery units, followed by electronics industries, have been dominating the composition of exports in these special enclaves. Currently, gems, jewellery and electronics together contribute almost 77 per cent of the total conventional exports of SEZs of the country. The maximum share is generated by the Santacruz SEZ, which is exclusively allowed to promote these two sectors. Despite having multi-product bases, the SEZs are influenced by the two sectors, namely gems and jewellery and electronics. This could also be one of the factors for the poor performance of Indian SEZs in comparison with their counterpart somewhere else. The sectoral concentration index (H_c) further substantiates our findings, as it has increased over the reference years, i.e., from 0.52 per cent in 1986–87 to 0.56 per cent in 2007–08 with a slight decline in the early 1990s (Figure 4.8). This indicates the growing vulnerability of Indian SEZs to fluctuations in the international market.

With respect to direction of SEZs trade, over the years USA has emerged as one of the prominent trade partners of the SEZs in India (Figure 4.9). This is especially due to changing sectoral composition of SEZ exports, which is dominated by the gems, jewellery and electronics, which is concentrated in USA market. The share of other countries, however, has reduced gradually from 59 per cent in 1990–91 to 38 per cent in 2007–08. Thus, contrary to the findings of Aggarwal (2004), which relate changes in the sectoral composition to changes in the trading partner of SEZs, our findings suggest that over the years, changes in the direction of exports have been in line with the changes in the sectoral composition of SEZ exports. This is because, as per comparative advantage theorem, a country tends to enter into international trade based upon its comparative advantage and factor endowments; whereas, the availability of international market alone does not determine the composition of exports, which is quite difficult at least in the short run. Thus, unless the government takes steps to diversify its exports, it would be quite difficult to diversify its reach in the international market. Furthermore, it is seen that due to a common sectoral composition of these enclaves, zones tend to compete with each other in the same international market, thereby presenting a different set of challenges to these enclaves domestically.

Besides trade promotion, employment generation and facilitating investment accumulation in the country are the other objectives of SEZs expansion in the country. Moreover, in the literature, employment generation through SEZs is considered as a mechanism to alleviate poverty (Engman et al., 2007), and investment as deciding factor of a spillover from these enclaves. As on 31 December 2014, over 3,22,481.55 crore have been invested in Indian SEZs and it also generated a direct employment of the order of 14 lakh persons so far.[15] However, the contribution of SEZs to the total organized employment in India is not very impressive. It accounted for just 1.04 per cent of the total organized employment in the country (Aggarwal, 2005). This could be due to the flawed sectoral composition of SEZs in the country. Therefore, there is a pressing need to promote these enclaves in such sectors, as that promises better employment generation.

Trade performance of SEZs in India – a disaggregate analysis[16]

Besides analysing the performance of SEZs in aggregate term, it is equally

---

15 The SEZ Board of Approval.

16 Originally published in *Margin—The Journal of Applied Economic Research*, Vol. 5, No. 2. Copyright © 2011 National Council of Applied Economic Research, New Delhi. All rights reserved. Reproduced with the permission of the copyright holders and the publishers, Sage Publications India Pvt. Ltd, New Delhi. However, substantial changes have been made in this section.

pertinent to explore performance of SEZs at the disaggregate level, given the government's efforts to promote an inclusive approach in achieving a balanced development. As these zones are considered engines of growth, variations, if any, in the performance across zones may further aggravate the problem of regional disparities in respect of development. Hence, in this section, we have attempted to explore the issue of performance of SEZs at the disaggregate level. Of the seven SEZs considered for the present analysis, a few zones are situated in the developed states whereas others either in the backward or less-developed states. Thus, it would be interesting to analyse whether zones located in developed states fare better than those located in partly or less-developed states, or whether there exist noticeable trends. The required information was obtained from the respective development commissioner's office of the select zones.

In order to record variations in the trade performance across zones and changes over the years, we constructed the zone-trade performance index (Z-TPI), similar to the index developed by ITC (2004) known as the trade performance index (TPI).[17] The need to construct an index to record variations in the performance of zones arose in view of the limitations of the existing set of studies. For instance, earlier studies (Kundra, 2000; Aggarwal, 2004 and 2005) have analysed the performance of SEZs at the disaggregate level based on trends in exports, import value and each zone's share in the total trade of SEZs. These studies, however, fail to analyse the issue in terms of a particular framework encompassing different performance parameters such as exporting units, sectoral concentration index, value addition, import-intensity of exports, and growth rates of exports and imports, which are equally important. Thus, there seems to be no basis for choosing performance parameters in their evaluation, resulting in only a partial picture of the complex scenario. Furthermore, the changes in performance before and after the introduction of the SEZ policy have not been explored by these studies.

---

17 Originally, TPI was constructed for assessing the various dimensions of export performance across countries in order to bring to the fore gains and losses in the global market, and also to the explore factors responsible for changes in their relative positions. It is a quantitative approach consisting of three types of indicators – a general profile, a given country position for the latest available year, and changes in the export performance in the recent years. This approach covers 184 countries and 14 different export sectors. In the present analysis, we have not followed the ITC approach (2004), though we have borrowed some ideas underlying this approach.

Approach to Z-TPI

Z-TPI was constructed based on 18 quantitative indicators (Table 4.4). The first five quantitative indicators provide a general profile (GP) of the zones, whereas the remaining 13 reveal the trade performance (TP) and its variations over the years. The index was computed for each indicator separately and, based on it, a composite index value for each zone was constructed for each period, ranging from zero to one. The closer the index values to one, the better the performance.

Table 4.4: A Brief on Components of Zone-Trade Performance Index (Z-TPI)

Indicator		Unit	Description and rationale
Indicators of a general profile			
G1	Geographical area	Acres	Total area of operation under each zone. This provides the variations in size across zones.
G2	Total exporting units	Numbers	Number of exporting units under each zone. This shows the changing interests of investors in a particular zone.
G3	Concentration of units	Ratio	Ratio of exporting units to the total geographical area. Against the exporting units, this captures the element of agglomeration/clustering of units.
G4	Employment	Person	Assesses the effectiveness of SEZs in generating employment opportunities.
G5	Investment	₹ crore*	Considers the total investment of these zones. Investment is considered as a channel to meet the expected benefits from these enclaves (Engman *et al.*, 2007).
Indicators of trade performance			
TP1	Total exports	₹ crore*	Gives the value of exports of each zone and changes over the years; it captures the capability of a given zone to meet the basic objective of promotion.
TP2	Total imports	₹ crore*	Value of imports and changes over the years

Indicator		Unit	Description and rationale
TP3	Net foreign exchange earnings	₹ crore*	Value of total net exports of each zone. As against value of exports, this shows which zone has added the maximum to the country's total SEZ-trade balance.
TP4	Value addition of SEZs	Ratio	Ratio of net foreign exchange earnings to the total exports of a zone; it gives the value addition by each zone.
TP5	Per capita exports	₹ crore*	Ratio of exports to exporting units; assesses the contribution of each additional exporting unit to the total value of exports.
TP6 and 7	Share in total exports and imports of SEZs	Per cent	Real contribution of each zone as against imports and exports.
TP8	Sectoral concentration index	Index	Computed based on Hirschman Sectoral Concentration Index; has a value between zero and one and captures export diversification.
TP9	Geographical concentration index	Index	Computed based on Hirschman Geographical Concentration Index; has a value between zero and one and captures the capability of zones in terms of reaching out to international markets.
TP10	Import intensity of exports	Ratio	Gives the import-content of exports – the imports required for exports as a percentage share of exports (Sathe, 1997), and takes on a value between one and hundred.
TP11 and 12	CAGR of exports and imports	Per cent	Locates the rate at which the performance parameters have changed in response to changes in policy.
TP13	Growth rate of exporting units	Per cent	Changing level of investor preference of a given a zone in accordance with changes in policy.

Source: Author's contribution.
Note: * Values are in ₹ crore at constant prices (1999–2000).

The indices computed for five different periods (Table 4.5) in respect to which data sets have been arranged in blocks of five years for the EPZ period and four years for the SEZs period.[18] The classification of time periods helps us locate changes in the performance of zones in response to policy changes over the two periods: the EPZ period (1986–87 to 1999–2000) and the SEZ period (2000–01 to 2007–08). This classification introduces an element of dynamism to the analysis in addition to providing three performance scenarios: (a) a general profile of each zone and changes over the years; (b) trade performance of each zone and changes over the years; and (c) relative changes in the general profile and trade performance across zones and over the entire period.

Table 4.5: Time Periods and Zones Covered for the Study

Time Period	Zones Covered
1986–87 to 1989–90	KSEZ, SSEZ, MSEZ, CSEZ, NSEZ, FSEZ
1990–91 to 1994–95	KSEZ, SSEZ, MSEZ, CSEZ, NSEZ, FSEZ
1995–96 to 1999–2000	KSEZ, SSEZ, MSEZ, CSEZ, NSEZ, FSEZ
2000–01 to 2003–04	KSEZ, SSEZ, MSEZ, CSEZ, NSEZ, FSEZ, VSEZ
2004–05 to 2007–08	KSEZ, SSEZ, MSEZ, CSEZ, NSEZ, FSEZ, VSEZ

Notes: The first three time periods under the classification capture the scenario of EPZs, while the fourth and the fifth capture the performance of SEZs. Due to limitations of data set, we have included Vizag SEZ only for the SEZ policy regime.

The index constructed is based on the minimum maximum approach advocated by Iyengar and Sudharshan (1982).[19]

$$Y_{it} = \frac{\text{Actual value in the series} - \text{Minimum value in the series}}{\text{Maximum value in the series} - \text{Minimum value in the series}}$$

However, if the indicator in question has a negative relation with performance, for instance, import intensity, then the equation can be rewritten as:

---

18 Average value of each reference period.

19 It is to be noted that Iyengar and Sudharshan (1982) originally proposed this technique in the early 1980s, which later, came to be known as the UNDP Maximum Minimum Approach in the computation of Human Development Indicators.

$$Y_{it} = \frac{\text{Maximum value in the series} - \text{Actual value in the series}}{\text{Maximum value in the series} - \text{Minimum value in the series}}$$

As against the general approach of assigning an equal weightage to all the indicators, Iyengar and Sudharshan (1982) assigned weights based on variations in each indicator. In the present analysis, we have followed the same procedure in that weights for each indicator and period are assigned separately (Tables 4.6 and 4.7).

$$W_i = \left[\frac{K}{\sqrt{\text{var}(y_i)}} \right]$$

In this,

$$K = \left[\frac{\sum 1}{\sqrt{\text{var}(y_i)}} \right]$$

Table 4.6: General Profile Indicators and Weights for Different Reference Periods

	1986–87 to 1989–90	1990–91 to 1994–95	1995–96 to 1999–2000	2000–01 to 2003–04	2004–05 to 2007–08
Area of zone	0.207	0.233	0.206	0.200	0.203
Exporting units	0.204	0.208	0.203	0.217	0.227
Density of units	0.210	0.245	0.213	0.198	0.198
Employment	0.180	0.207	0.207	0.203	0.198
Investment	0.199	0.108	0.171	0.182	0.175

Source: Author's estimation.

Table 4.7: Trade Performance Indicators and Weights for Different Reference Periods

	1986–87 to 1989–90	1990–91 to 1994–95	1995–96 to 1999–2000	2000–01 to 2003–04	2004–05 to 2007–08
Total exports	0.079	0.081	0.076	0.078	0.076
Total imports	0.074	0.080	0.074	0.077	0.063
Net foreign exchange earnings	0.086	0.074	0.075	0.079	0.087

	1986–87 to 1989–90	1990–91 to 1994–95	1995–96 to 1999–2000	2000–01 to 2003–04	2004–05 to 2007–08
Value addition by SEZs	0.089	0.064	0.081	0.076	0.082
Per capita exports	0.084	0.080	0.078	0.062	0.078
Share in the total exports of SEZs	0.080	0.079	0.076	0.078	0.075
Share in imports	0.076	0.080	0.074	0.077	0.068
Sectoral concentration index	0.082	0.073	0.083	0.063	0.063
Geographical concentration index	NA	0.074	0.069	0.074	0.060
Import intensity of exports	0.094	0.064	0.081	0.076	0.082
CAGR of exports	0.085	0.079	0.079	0.087	0.086
CAGR of imports	0.092	0.082	0.079	0.087	0.087
Growth rate of exporting units	0.078	0.089	0.075	0.086	0.093

Source: Author's estimation.

Furthermore, in order to test the statistical significance of the variations in performance across zones, a one-way analysis of variance (ANOVA) has been conducted with respect to the TPI of all seven zones for the entire reference period.

Zone-level variations in performance – results and discussion

As stated above, based on the average value of each indicator and the period under investigation (Annexure Tables 4.1 and 4.2), two separate indices have been computed, namely, the general profile index and TPI. Table 4.8 presents a general profile index of the zones over the reference periods, and we have ranked them on the basis of value of this index in Table 4.9. Tables 4.10 and 4.11 depict the TPI and its ranking, respectively.

Table 4.8: General Profile Index of Zones over the Reference Periods

	KSEZ	SEEZ	MSEZ	CSEZ	NSEZ	FSEZ	VSEZ
1986–87 to 1989–90	0.80	0.37	0.18	0.11	0.36	0.27	NE
1990–91 to 1994–95	0.68	0.49	0.12	0.37	0.57	0.37	NA
1995–96 to 1999–2000	0.62	0.46	0.27	0.13	0.55	0.36	NA

	KSEZ	SEEZ	MSEZ	CSEZ	NSEZ	FSEZ	VSEZ
2000–01 to 2003–04	0.63	0.53	0.32	0.21	0.45	0.19	0.31
2004–05 to 2007–08	0.55	0.60	0.16	0.28	0.37	0.21	0.39

Source: Author's estimation.
Note: NE indicates 'not established'; NA indicates 'not available'.

Table 4.9: General Profile Ranking Position of Zones over the Reference Periods

Rank	1986–87 to 1989–90	1990–91 to 1994–95	1995–96 to 1999–2000	2000–01 to 2003–04	2004–05 to 2007–08
1	KSEZ	SSEZ	SSEZ	SSEZ	SSEZ
2	FSEZ	NSEZ	CSEZ	NSEZ	NSEZ
3	NSEZ	KSEZ	KSEZ	KSEZ	CSEZ
4	SSEZ	MSEZ	NSEZ	FSEZ	MSEZ
5	CSEZ	CSEZ	MSEZ	MSEZ	KSEZ
6	MSEZ	FSEZ	FSEZ	CSEZ	VSEZ
7	--	--	--	VSEZ	FSEZ

Source: Author's compilation based on Table 4.8.

Table 4.10: Trade Performance Index of Zones over the Reference Periods

Time period	KSEZ	SEEZ	MSEZ	CSEZ	NSEZ	FSEZ	VSEZ
1986–87 to 1989–90	0.52	0.36	0.16	0.29	0.38	0.41	NE
1990–91 to 1994–95	0.35	0.69	0.31	0.25	0.51	0.22	NA
1995–96 to 1999–2000	0.32	0.67	0.26	0.23	0.42	0.28	NA
2000–01 to 2003–04	0.39	0.75	0.31	0.25	0.43	0.37	0.14
2004–05 to 2007–08	0.42	0.58	0.47	0.51	0.54	0.21	0.29

Note: NE indicates 'not established' and NA indicates 'not available'.
Source: Author's estimation.

**Table 4.11: Trade Performance Ranking Position of Zones
over the Reference Periods**

Rank	1986–87 to 1989–90	1990–91 to 1994–95	1995–96 to 1999–2000	2000–01 to 2003–04	2004–05 to 2007–08
1	KSEZ	SSEZ	SSEZ	SSEZ	SSEZ
2	NSEZ	NSEZ	NSEZ	FSEZ	NSEZ
3	SSEZ	KSEZ	KSEZ	KSEZ	CSEZ
4	FSEZ	CSEZ	MSEZ	NSEZ	KSEZ and MSEZ
5	CSEZ	FSEZ	FSEZ	MSEZ	FSEZ and VSEZ
6	MSEZ	MSEZ	CSEZ	CSEZ	
7				VSEZ	

Source: Author's compilation based on Table 4.10.

Instead of explaining the variations in performance across zones and over the years, based on the absolute value of indices (in Tables 4.8 and 4.10) and subsequent rankings (Tables 4.9 and 4.11) in the present context, we have evaluated the performance of zones in two different ways. Initially, zones are categorized under a threefold classification based on the ranking of each zone for the latest reference period (2004–05 to 2007–08) over the rankings of zones for the base period (1986–97 to 1989–90). Here, the first classification represents zones whose status has remained unchanged over the entire reference period. The second and third classifications comprise zones that show an improvement and deterioration, respectively, in their performance. These categorizations help to explain how each zone has responded over the years to policy changes and its performance *vis-à-vis* other zones.

Table 4.12: Performance Evaluation of Zones – I

Ranking	General profile	Trade performance
Performance unchanged	---	---
Performance improved/gainer	SSEZ and CSEZ	SSEZ, NSEZ, CSEZ and MSEZ
Performance deteriorated	NSEZ KSEZ and FSEZ and MSEZ	KSEZ and FSEZ

Source: Author's calculation based on tables 4.8, 4.9, 4.10 and 4.11.

Table 4.13: Performance Evaluation of Zones – II

Ranking	General profile	Trade performance
Better performing zone (2007–08)	SSEZ and KSEZ	SSEZ and NSEZ
Poor performing zone (2007–08)	CSEZ, FSEZ and MSEZ	FSEZ and VSEZ

Source: Author's calculation based on tables 4.8, 4.9, 4.10 and 4.11.

The above performance evaluation, however, fails to provide the position and ranking for each zone for the latest reference period, i.e., 2004–05 to 2007–08, in relation to other zones. Therefore, in Table 4.13, we have evaluated the performance of zones under two sub-categories: better-performing and poor-performing zones. The following subsection presents a discussion of these issues.

General profile index of zones

Based on the evaluation of the performance of zones, measured with the help of five indicators, it emerges that, barring Santacruz and Cochin, all SEZs show a deterioration under the two different policy regimes (Tables 4.9 and 4.12). Of the seven zones, Kandla is found to have benefited through an expansion in its area from 700 acres to 1,000 acres (Appendix Tables 4.1 and 4.2), in view of its being able to attract new units with a relatively larger area for operation. Surprisingly, despite its improved position in terms of increased number of exporting units (among the seven zones), it has failed to attract investment from the private sector, foreign investors and non-resident Indians in companion with other zones. At the same time, it also has failed to generate adequate employment opportunities besides slipping slightly in its ranking. The deterioration in the ranking of Falta SEZ is due to its failure to improve its position in respect of any of the general profile indicators, barring an improvement in the number of its exporting units. Santacruz SEZ, however, has improved its position due to an increase growth in the number of total exporting units and, thereby, in total investment and employment generation. Similarly, improvements in Cochin SEZ could also be explained by the same reasoning.

Trade performance index

The trade performance of the zones, measured through 13 independent indicators, reveals a slight change in the position of all the zones under the two policy regimes – the EPZ and SEZ (Table 4.11). For instance, an increase in the index value of NSEZ from 0.38 per cent (1986–87 to 1989–90) to 0.54 per cent (2003–04 to 2007–08). For the same period, the index value of Santacruz, Cochin and Madras SEZs shows an increase from 0.36, 0.29 and 0.16 per cent to 0.58, 0.51 and 0.47 per cent, respectively. However, over the same period, the trade performance of Kandla and Falta SEZs has deteriorated from 0.52 to 0.42 per cent, whereas the improvement in Noida SEZ performance is mainly because of an improvement in its share in the total imports of SEZs. Santacruz SEZ, however, has succeeded in improving its position through a higher growth rate of its exporting units and a reduced import intensity of exports. Cochin SEZ has managed to push itself up through a higher value of exports, imports and per capita exports, while improving its position at the national level. This could be mainly due to an improvement in its share in the total exports and imports of SEZs which, in turn, eventually lead to an improvement in its aggregate growth rates of exports and imports. Madras (Chennai) SEZ has improved its performance through an increased geographical diversification of exports, and higher growth rates of exports, imports and exporting units. The higher sectoral and geographical concentration along with reduced growth rates of exports and imports during the SEZ period has led to deterioration in the position of Falta SEZ *vis-à-vis* other zones. Even its reduced geographical concentration is found ineffective in improving the overall position of Falta SEZ. The deteriorating position of Kandla could be attributed to a lower value of exports and imports relative to other zones and hence, a lower growth rate in exports and imports.

The introduction of the SEZ policy (2000–01) in place of the conventional EPZ structure has had a positive impact on the performance of all the seven zones under study. Meanwhile, it is interesting to note that Kandla, Falta and Cochin zones show a dip in performance from 1990–91 to 1995–96 in relation to their performance in the previous period (Table 4.8). This could be due to the disintegration of the USSR, a major trading partner of these enclaves. For instance, the export value of KSEZ falling from ₹ 400 crore in 1990–91 to ₹ 90 crore in 1995–96. A similar trend is noticed for FSEZ. Furthermore, with the exception of FSEZ, all the other zones show a decline in performance between 1995–96 and 1999–2000 following the East Asian crisis. For instance, the fall of MSEZ export value from ₹ 1,020 crore in 1996–97 to ₹ 268 crore in 1998–99. Moreover, in 2010 (January 6), the Board of Approvals accepted the denotification requests from 10 SEZ developers who had been adversely affected by the global downturn and the subsequent decline in demand for domestic goods and services. These, taken together, further substantiate our argument that, despite their status as separate economic entities with privileged benefits, these enclaves are equally susceptible to the changing fortunes of the world economy. Towards mitigating such challenges, the sectoral composition as well as geographical diversification of SEZs seems to have played a decisive role in their success. For instance, the disintegration of the USSR did not have a negative impact on the performance of Santacruz, Noida and Chennai SEZs, in view of their well-diversified sectoral composition. This, in turn, also helped determine their trading partners.

Although an analysis of the absolute index value reveals variations in the performance across zones; however, to find out the statistical significance of variations in the performance, as identified in the above exercise, we have carried out a one-way ANOVA for TPI value. The result, presented in Table 4.14, rejects the null hypothesis, that is, 'there exists no significant variation in the trade performance across the seven zones', while supporting the alternative hypothesis that there exist significant variations in the performance across zones.

Table 4.14: ANOVA for Trade Performance Index

Source of variation	SS	df	MS	F
Between groups	0.379	5	0.075	6.73
Within groups	0.27	24	0.011	
Total	0.65	29		

Source: Author's estimation.
Note: F value is significant at 1 per cent level.

Of the seven zones, Santacruz and Noida have been performing relatively better than the rest, whereas Vizag and Falta find themselves at the bottom of performance rankings. This, in turn, implies that zones[20] located in the better-performing states[21] (SSEZ, NSEZ) have recorded relatively better

---

20 Parameters of better-performing zones have already been discussed above in great detail.

21 In the literature, we find the performance of states usually measured and categorized as better and poor based on NSDP, per capita income, sectoral composition, infrastructure availability and investment ratio. Following the criteria, we find

performances as compared to zones in other states (FSEZ, VSEZ), indicating thereby that the problem of regional disparities is reflected in the performance of SEZs as well. However, one may challenge this view by claiming that SEZs are not being promoted with the objective of achieving a balanced development in the country, but as growth centres for developing linkages with the rest of the economy in the course of time. The global experience in this respect is inconclusive. For instance, despite a commanding performance of China's SEZs in achieving the objectives behind their promotion, they are often held responsible for creating regional disparities in development.[22]

In the Indian context, most of the upcoming SEZs are planned to be located in the developed states. For instance, Maharashtra, Andhra Pradesh, Tamil Nadu and Karnataka have received more approvals for SEZs than the other states. Such concentration of zones in few states/region may pose two types of threats to the promotion of a balanced development. First, developed states continue to receive a lion's share in the SEZ approvals in the country, which can further widen the existing disparities between the developed and developing states, since regions with SEZs tend to receive more attention. This could result in the depletion of the natural resource base of the surrounding regions, more in terms of a backwash effect rather than a spread effect. Second, the concentration of zones in a given region may exhaust its resource base, resulting in diseconomies of scale and congestion, which, in turn, may possibly throw up a completely different set of challenges. Thus, if proper attention is not paid to the potential threats of SEZs expansion, it might in the long run, aggravate further the regional disparities in India.

The present analysis also helps us argue that the size of a given zone is not the sole criterion in terms of determining its overall profile and performance. For instance, geographically larger zones (Kandla and Vizag) have failed in generating sufficient employment opportunities and investment. This may be due to location, the number of exporting units or the type of industry being promoted within these zones. Santacruz SEZ, however, though smaller in

---

Maharashtra consistently ranked among the developed states of the Indian economy. In fact, Maharashtra as registered a remarkable 8 per cent growth in the post-reform period (Ahluwalia, 2000) with its per capita income being constantly higher over the years *vis-á-vis* the national average. In contrast, Uttar Pradesh registers very poor performance in the post-reform period, but finds itself ranked first in terms of investment ratio. In fact, it is above the national average (Ahluwalia, 2000).

22 Refer chapter 3 for further discussion on this.

size, ranks first in terms of the number of exporting units and employment and investment generation (Annexure Tables 4.1 and 4.2). This could be particularly attributed to the pre-eminence of the gems and jewellery sectors operating within the zone, which enjoy a better scope in terms of providing adequate employment opportunities for both the skilled and semi-skilled labour. In the trade sphere too, Kandla and Vizag SEZs occupy the fifth and seventh positions, respectively. However, Santacruz SEZ, followed by Noida SEZs are found outperforming other SEZs, under the same policy regime. The Vizag SEZ experience reveals that, though it continues to remain the least preferred destination for investors (exporting units), in terms of volume it ranks second in the current SEZ period (2004–05 to 2007–08). This could be due to the presence of companies such as Dr Reddy's Laboratory, LID Diamonds, etc. The performance of Noida SEZ, however, points to the fact that proximity to seaport or airport is neither a sufficient nor necessary condition for the success of SEZs. However, the above inference cannot be generalized in the absence of other supportive conditions and this needs further exploration.

Summary

A performance analysis of SEZs on the basis of aggregate indicators reveals that the introduction of the SEZ policy has had a positive and significant impact on the functional dimensions of these enclaves. Although the performance of SEZs in terms of their share in the country's aggregate trade presents an optimistic picture, yet it is not comparable to SEZs of other countries. At the same, it is important to note here that it is the general macro-economic structure and the prevailing business environment of the economy that significantly shape the overall functioning of these zones. Stated otherwise, there exists a bidirectional relation between the performance of SEZs and the macro-economy.

More importantly, these enclaves are observed to be highly sensitive to changes in the global economy either in terms of a slowdown or inflation. The capacity to withstand such global fluctuations depends on how well the trade baskets of SEZs are diversified in terms of product composition and trading partners. Thus, along with building up of a trade-related infrastructure base in the context of SEZs, it is equally important to diversify the exports basket of these enclaves, which may require a more elaborate macro-economic policy response. Besides that the SEZ policy in the present context has not been very successful so far in diversifying the exports basket. As aptly remarked by Kundra: 'instead of establishing multi-product SEZs, the State should promote two or three product-based SEZs' (2000, 74) from the view point of both efficiency and cost. Thus, instead of directing and assessing these SEZs on the basis of policy objectives, their development and performance should be guided by the existing comparative advantages (Wong, 1987). The most important task to be undertaken, in this regard, relates to the identification of each region's comparative advantage in factor endowment and production process. Theoretically also, exports to be promoted from a region and/or an attempt to attract foreign investment should reflect the factor endowment or else it may result in an under-utilization of resources due to the non-availability of the required factors at reasonable costs and other supportive mechanisms. Moreover, unless the government takes serious steps to diversify its exports, it would be difficult to expand its reach in the international market as well. This could make these enclaves more susceptible to changes in the world economy either in the form of recession and/or inflation. A scrutiny of the newly approved SEZs in the country further mirrors the mal-adjustment not only in terms of sectoral composition but also SEZ approvals across the states. Although it is quite apparent that the developed states continue to receive maximum approvals and backward states are struggling to attract the attention of investors. This indicates at the problem of regional disparities which may get further aggravated in future if adequate corrective measures are not initiated. Disaggregate analysis reveals that variations are found in performance across the seven SEZs. In fact, it is observed that the relatively better-performing zones are those that are located in developed states rather than in less-developed states. This indicates that regional disparity is not only reflected in SEZ performance, but also that they could hardly address such imbalance. Furthermore, the intensity of problems is likely to be magnified considering the concentration of newly notified SEZs in a few regions within a few developed states. Third, despite their status as separate economic entities with privileges and benefits not available to rest of the economy, these enclaves were equally susceptible to changing fortunes of the world economy.

Annexure

Annexure Table 4.1: Average Value of Z-TPI Indicators for EPZ Policy Regime

	KSEZ			SEEPZ			MSEZ			CSEZ			NSEZ			FSEZ		
	1986–87 to 1989–90	1990–91 to 1994–95	1995–96 to 1999–2000	1986–87 to 1989–90	1990–91 to 1994–95	1995–96 to 1999–2000	1986–87 to 1989–90	1990–91 to 1994–95	1995–96 to 1999–2000	1986–87 to 1989–90	1990–91 to 1994–95	1995–96 to 1999–2000	1986–87 to 1989–90	1990–91 to 1994–95	1995–1996 to 1999–2000	1986–87 to 1989–90	1990–91 to 1994–95	1995–96 to 1999–2000
General profile indicators																		
G1. Area of zone																		
Values (acres)	700.00	700.00	700.00	104.00	104.00	104.00	103.00	103.00	103.00	103.00	103.00	103.00	310.00	310.00	310.00	280.00	280.00	280.00
G2. Exporting units																		
Values (units)	130.50	126.20	131.60	80.25	127.20	155.40	29.50	75.00	89.20	4.25	21.80	41.00	20.75	85.40	119.60	2.25	15.20	49.20
G3. Density of units																		
Values (units)	5.37	5.58	5.36	1.31	0.84	0.67	6.83	1.41	1.18	49.55	4.93	2.59	24.41	3.97	2.69	180.83	21.66	6.69
G4. Employment																		
Values (units)	9187.50	9300.00	10126.80	8625.00	14200.00	26783.80	1560.00	8135.00	16223.40	727.00	3831.00	4889.20	2250.00	6164.80	15597.00	90.00	937.00	1940.20
G5. Investment																		
Values (₹ crore)*	25.09	18.85	32.45	9.57	14.58	15.63	13.50	5.70	10.87	5.50	15.30	10.88	24.25	36.40	49.80	0.37	5.32	45.91
Trade performance indicators																		
TP1. Total exports																		
Values (₹ crore)*	611.86	522.00	447.75	399.74	1279.56	2918.87	46.58	242.54	737.07	12.49	80.62	188.88	54.40	254.42	681.23	14.48	42.70	89.42
TP2. Total imports																		
Values (₹ crore)*	357.87	238.23	128.21	302.41	899.26	1470.93	41.02	163.55	553.17	11.87	53.35	116.93	31.70	96.61	347.32	5.03	20.96	65.70
TP3. Net foreign exchange earnings																		
Values (₹ crore)*	253.99	283.77	319.54	97.33	380.30	1447.94	5.56	78.99	183.91	0.62	27.27	71.95	22.70	157.82	333.91	9.45	21.74	23.71

contd...

contd...

	KSEZ			SEEPZ			MSEZ			CSEZ			NSEZ			FSEZ		
	1986–87 to 1989–90	1990–91 to 1994–95	1995–96 to 1999–2000	1986–87 to 1989–90	1990–91 to 1994–95	1995–96 to 1999–2000	1986–87 to 1989–90	1990–91 to 1994–95	1995–96 to 1999–2000	1986–87 to 1989–90	1990–91 to 1994–95	1995–96 to 1999–2000	1986–87 to 1989–90	1990–91 to 1994–95	1995–96 to 1999–2000	1986–87 to 1989–90	1990–91 to 1994–95	1995–96 to 1999–2000
TP4. Value addition of SEZs																		
Values (ratio)	0.42	0.58	0.71	0.26	0.30	0.48	0.13	0.24	0.28	0.25	0.25	0.38	0.52	0.56	0.48	0.60	0.50	-0.43
TP5. Per capita exports																		
Values (₹ crore)*	4.69	4.06	3.41	4.88	9.75	18.85	2.81	2.73	5.85	3.60	3.44	4.63	2.34	3.14	8.66	5.41	3.36	1.52
TP6. Share in total exports of SEZs																		
Values (per cent)	54.42	24.05	8.81	33.96	51.51	56.03	4.05	9.84	14.68	1.02	3.12	3.66	4.43	9.73	13.29	1.08	1.85	1.54
TP7. Share in imports of SEZs																		
Values (per cent)	49.73	18.13	4.72	39.22	59.08	54.08	5.43	11.40	19.88	1.34	3.54	4.32	3.79	6.38	12.80	0.48	1.49	2.49
TP8. Sectoral concentration index																		
Values (percentage)	0.55	0.72	0.54	1.00	0.74	0.72	0.86	0.53	0.53	1.00	0.71	0.50	0.19	0.58	0.43	1.00	0.76	0.59
TP9. Geographical concentration index																		
Values (percentage)	NA	0.94	0.67	NA	0.60	0.54	NA	0.58	0.60	NA	NA	NA	NA	0.61	0.52	NA	NA	0.78
TP10. Import intensity of exports																		
Values (per cent)	58.40	42.27	28.81	74.36	69.87	52.03	87.20	76.04	72.32	74.95	74.53	62.31	48.17	43.93	51.33	14.63	50.17	64.12
TP11. CAGR of exports																		
Values (per cent)	5.97	1.00	1.00	32.05	0.02	0.25	31.78	0.05	0.00	100.97	0.00	0.06	71.94	0.96	0.23	NA	NA	0.26
TP12. CAGR imports																		
Values (per cent)	5.97	0.00	0.12	32.05	0.48	0.28	31.78	0.48	0.00	100.97	1.00	0.22	71.94	0.75	0.19	169.12	NA	1.00
TP13. Growth rate of exporting units																		
Values (per cent)	3.98	0.00	0.12	9.09	0.48	0.28	108.13	0.48	0.00	117.28	1.00	0.22	90.22	0.75	0.19	69.22	NA	1.00

Source: Author's estimation based on the data collected from DC offices of respective zones.
Note: NA, not available.
*Values are in ₹ crore at constant prices (1999–2000).

Annexure

Annexure Table 4.2: Average Value of Z-TPI Indicators for SEZs Policy Regime

	KSEZ		SEEPZ		MSEZ		CSEZ		NSEZ		FSEZ		VSEZ	
	2000–01 to 2003–04	2004–05 to 2007–08	2000–01 to 2003–04	2004–05 to 2007–08	2000–01 to 2003–04	2004–05 to 2007–08	2000–01 to 2003–04	2004–05 to 2007–08	2000–01 to 2003–04	2004–05 to 2007–08	2000–01 to 2003–04	2004–05 to 2007–08	2000–01 to 2003–04	2004–05 to 2007–08
General profile indicators														
G1. Area of zone														
Values (acres)	1000.00	1000.00	104.00	104.00	103.00	103.00	103.00	103.00	310.00	310.00	280.00	280.00	360.00	360.00
G2. Exporting units														
Values (units)	127.75	158.50	192.00	284.00	85.00	108.50	55.50	79.00	124.25	157.75	126.50	117.50	18.00	34.50
G3. Density of units														
Values (units)	7.96	6.36	0.60	0.37	1.22	0.95	1.92	1.31	2.53	1.97	2.23	2.52	20.25	10.67
G4. Employment														
Values (units)	9750.00	14650.50	39500.00	44137.50	12997.25	20631.00	4966.00	7703.00	14383.75	28112.50	2821.75	3816.00	2837.00	3052.00
G5. Investment														
Values (₹ crore)*	30.88	24.62	21.20	35.21	29.91	18.25	24.30	37.19	31.17	24.47	5.83	22.91	13.27	30.96
Trade performance indicators														
TP1. Total exports														
Values (₹ crore)*	641.15	1080.66	4855.45	6144.13	730.15	1669.32	285.73	1632.79	1005.32	4609.07	629.18	426.61	902.31	1229.09
TP2. Total imports														
Values (₹ crore)	251.34	403.63	2812.81	3706.24	557.46	1133.00	160.77	1175.88	424.73	3689.90	109.18	159.99	481.65	1270.03
TP3. Net foreign exchange earnings														
Values (₹ crore)*	389.81	677.03	2042.64	2437.89	172.69	536.32	124.97	456.91	580.59	919.17	520.00	266.61	420.66	-40.94
TP4. Value addition of SEZs														
Values (ratio)	0.62	0.63	0.42	0.40	0.25	0.31	0.43	0.37	0.58	0.20	0.82	0.62	0.23	-0.15

contd...

contd...

	KSEZ		SEEPZ		MSEZ		CSEZ		NSEZ		FSEZ		VSEZ	
	2000–01 to 2003–04	2004–05 to 2007–08	2000–01 to 2003–04	2004–05 to 2007–08	2000–01 to 2003–04	2004–05 to 2007–08	2000–01 to 2003–04	2004–05 to 2007–08	2000–01 to 2003–04	2004–05 to 2007–08	2000–01 to 2003–04	2004–05 to 2007–08	2000–01 to 2003–04	2004–05 to 2007–08
TP5. Per capita exports														
Values (₹ crore)*	4.96	6.79	28.20	21.62	8.14	29.12	5.24	20.29	8.58	15.31	4.97	3.80	25.40	35.19
TP6. Share in total exports														
Values (per cent)	7.10	6.47	53.88	37.73	8.13	9.85	3.16	8.96	11.11	27.66	7.08	2.66	9.73	7.24
TP7. Share in imports														
Values (per cent)	5.07	3.47	58.54	32.96	11.32	9.63	3.57	8.81	8.98	32.37	2.32	1.37	10.20	11.39
TP8. Sectoral concentration index														
Values (per cent)	0.68	0.53	0.71	0.79	0.46	0.44	0.62	0.50	0.46	0.69	0.57	0.60	NA	NA
TP9. Geographical concentration index														
Values (per cent)	0.65	0.62	0.60	0.74	0.63	0.57	NA	NA	0.54	0.53	0.77	0.74	NA	NA
TP10. Import intensity of exports														
Values (per cent)	38.26	37.12	57.98	60.23	74.83	68.70	56.76	63.35	42.34	80.10	18.04	37.85	77.37	115.13
TP11. CAGR of exports														
Values (per cent)	23.99	19.96	3.25	6.08	9.75	28.15	6.08	81.12	8.22	18.41	6.61	-1.78	-37.50	32.98
TP12. CAGR imports														
Values (per cent)	23.99	19.96	3.25	6.08	9.75	28.15	6.08	81.12	8.22	18.41	6.61	-1.78	-37.50	23.99
TP13. Growth rate of exporting units														
Values (per cent)	10.52	6.82	28.02	1.92	1.71	1.92	14.11	3.15	-3.44	1.82	8.44	-6.29	9.31	13.88

Source: Author's estimation based on the data collected from DC offices of respective zones.

Note: NA, not available.

*Values are in ₹ crore at constant prices (1999–2000).

5

An Assessment of the Fiscal Viability of
Special Economic Zones

Background

The rationale underlying the liberalization process is guided by the assumption that its spillover effects would benefit the domestic economy (mainly through accelerating the pace of economic growth) and that the resultant benefits would trickle down to all segments of the economy. In this respect, there seems to be general consensus regarding the potential of trade reform measures in terms of boosting economic growth *vis-à-vis* the initial restrictive trade regime. Yet, there are certain concerns voiced about the rationale behind the reform process. The most common concern about various aspects of trade reform measures is related to the possible effects on the fiscal situation of the economy, particularly the revenue front of the government which, in turn, may pose challenges to the government's efforts towards meeting the various social welfare schemes. This is considered the prime reason for resource constraints, which most of the developing economies have been facing in the post-liberalization period, following a substantial drop in the tax revenues. The empirical evidence in this respect seems to be both inconclusive and ambiguous in nature.[1]

Nevertheless, given the additional burden that these measures are likely to place on the fiscal health of the economy, understanding the impacts of trade policy reform measures on the fiscal position of the country seems necessary in view of their known influence on the distributional aspect. In this context,

---

1   See for details: Ebrill *et al.* (1999); Matlanyane and Harmse (2002); Zafar (2005); Stiglitz and Charlton (2005); Soni *et al.* (2007)

Greenway and Milner (1991)[2] identify two sets of factors that explain how different dimensions of reform measures may affect the domestic economy in various ways. One is based on the initial economic conditions of the economy. If a country is highly insulated and underdeveloped, then exposure to the world market through trade measures can have adverse effects on the revenue sources, particularly through a substantial reduction in tax revenues. Two, the reforms undertaken depend on the measures adopted to smoothen out the reform process. If a policy initiative is directed by quantitative restrictions on import tariffs and/or replacement of duty exemption with lower tariff rates, then there is a possibility of its increasing the revenue source of income. On the contrary, if policy initiatives are oriented towards gradually reducing import tariffs, by way of offering special incentives to any particular section of the society in the form of substantial tax concessions, tax exemptions, etc., there is every possibility of having some negative impact on the fiscal position of the economy at least in the short run. However, there is a counter-argument that a reduction in tax rates could increase demand for imports besides reducing the extent of corruption at different levels of bureaucracy as also smuggling due to reduced rates of import tariff (Greenway and Milner, 1991). In the context of trade reforms, the fiscal situation of a country becomes more crucial considering the additional responsibilities to be taken up by governments in order to facilitate trade.

In the context of the Indian economy, the process of reforms in the trade sphere began with a gradual dismantling of quantitative restrictions along with lowering of import tax rates. On an average, tariff rates in India were reduced from 128.0 per cent in 1990–91 to 39.6 per cent in 1999–2000 (Ahulwalia, 2009). As a result, the tax revenue showed signs of a decline during the post-1990s. Hence, this issue is increasingly drawing the attention of policymakers as also academicians in terms of its possible impact on the fiscal situation of the economy. Specifically, this has gained further prominence in the recent past consequent upon the introduction and gradual spread of the most ambitious trade measure of the government, under the banner of special economic zone (SEZ) policy. This policy has resulted not only in the reduction of tax rates, but

---

2 This has been based on a case study of five countries covered under Structural Adjustment Lending of the World Bank.

also the withdrawal of major taxes by both the central and state governments.[3] Notably, these taxes constitute the main revenue source for both the central and state governments. This is quite an extreme scenario, as explained by Greenway and Milner (1991) because, in the SEZ policy framework, the role envisaged for these zones and the enthusiasm with which the government has promoted them notwithstanding, their creation and maintenance seem to be affecting the national exchequer in two ways. First, given the expenditure involved in creating separate institutional arrangements for reducing the cumbersome bureaucratic procedures and creating world-class infrastructure facilities, the government is clearly and steadfastly playing the role of a trade facilitator. Second, in its role as a fiscal manager, the government suffers a considerable loss of revenue by providing fiscal incentives in terms of tax concessions and subsidies. In other words, the establishment and sustenance of SEZs tend to cause an additional revenue and capital expenditure, on the one hand and a massive revenue loss, on the other.

Given these factors, while assessing the growth of SEZs and acknowledging their contribution to trade expansion, employment generation and increased private investment, it is imperative that we consider the costs involved in the promotion of such ventures, especially the enormous stress they apparently exert on the fiscal health of the economy. In the recent past, there has been a debate going on among observers of SEZs concerning the issue of costs associated with the promotion of these enclaves (see Aggarwal, 2007; Mukhopadhay, 2007; Rao, 2007).[4] This debate, surprisingly, seems focused on questioning the very legitimacy of attempts to examine the costs associated with the expansion of SEZs, as if it is to be taken for granted. Although there are proponents of the view that outflow from the national exchequer and the recurring revenue loss need to be examined in detail, however, very little in the form of an appropriate methodology has come from these quarters. It is against this background that we look into the fiscal viability issue of SEZs in the Indian context in this chapter.

---

3   For details, see chapter 2.

4   This is mainly due to the resource crunch that the government is facing in the implementation of most of the development projects, on the one hand and also the backdrop of the fear that SEZs are perhaps leading a realignment of investment from domestic tariff areas (DTA) to SEZs rather than promoting fresh investments in the economy.

Conceptual and analytical frameworks for quantifying the fiscal viability of SEZs

The fiscal implications of SEZs analysed in the present context are labelled as resource cost and is defined as those costs which, in the process of generating Net Foreign Exchange, negatively impact the fiscal situation of the economy either directly or indirectly, in the short or long run. The fiscal implications of SEZs, as defined above, could be brought under a two-fold classification (Chart 5.1). First, those that have a direct and immediate (short-term) impact on the fiscal position of the economy. This further consists of two components, that is, those that lead to a loss of revenue to the government exchequer and those that contribute significantly to an additional expenditure on the part of the government. The second encompasses those that have an indirect impact on the budgetary position of the economy not only in the short run but also the long run. Thus, the term 'resource cost' could be understood in a boarder sense for capturing the direct impact of the promotion of SEZs on the fiscal position of the economy (a reduction in the tax revenue and a substantial increase in the expenditure of the government). It can also be used for capturing the indirect impact on the budgetary position of the economy, in the long and short term (see Table 5.1 for various components of resource costs and the projected benefits of SEZs). For instance, for promoting SEZs in India, private lands have been acquired in rural areas for many of the upcoming projects. In respect of such acquisitions, although a monetary compensation is paid at the prevailing market price, alternative employment opportunities are not provided. Further, those displaced by land acquisition are generally left to fend for themselves. This, in turn, necessitates government intervention at different levels in terms of rehabilitating and resettling the displaced people, which will eventually, put an additional burden on the fiscal position of the economy. Furthermore, the possible fiscal implications of the SEZ policy depend on the way the policy is designed and executed. Thus, *ceteris paribus*, we assume *a priori* that fiscal implications of SEZs, like fiscal implications of trade policy measures, depend on the following factors.

Chart 5.1: Resource Cost and SEZs

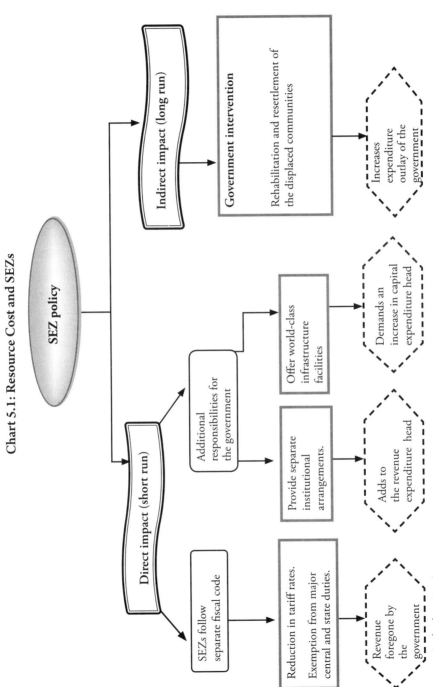

Source: Author's estimation.

Table 5.1: Components of Resource Costs and Projected Benefits of SEZ Expansion

Sl No	Components	Description
		Resource Costs
1	Administrative costs	The government incurs a high expenditure on the maintenance of separate administrative offices in each zone, which eventually adds to the revenue expenditure of the government budget.
2	Maintenance costs	If zones are owned and funded by the government, then all expenditure on the development of plots, infrastructure facilities and their maintenance have to be borne by the central government which increases the expenditure of the government budget known as 'capital expenditure'[i].
3	Revenue foregone	To attract investors to these zones, especially foreign direct investment, both the central and state governments have formulated a separate fiscal code for these enclaves. The code allows a substantial reduction in tax rates, a number of tax concessions as well as subsidies to different actors involved in the promotion of SEZs. These incentives, however, differ across zones. The tax concessions and subsidies have a direct impact on the fiscal position of the economy in terms of a substantial loss of revenue to the government exchequer, at least in the short run.
4	Indirect costs	SEZs can adversely affect the economy indirectly. This, in turn, necessitates government intervention at different levels to address the imbalance. Such indirect costs are long term in nature and may not be realized/understood in the short run. The major ones include the cost of government intervention at different layers to protect the fundamental rights of people affected, cost of rehabilitation and resettlement of the displaced and addressing the negative externalities generated in the process and others.
		Proposed benefits
1	Foreign exchange earnings	The foremost benefit expected from these zones is the generation of foreign exchange earnings. The apparent reason for focusing on SEZs to generate foreign exchange earnings is their presumed innate capacity to generate spillover effects on the domestic economy in addition to earning foreign exchange.

Sl No	Components	Description
2	Employment generation	Besides promoting exports, these zones are expected to generate employment opportunities on the domestic front to address the broader development objective of a nation state.
3	Private and foreign investments	Besides export earning and employment promotion, investments are considered as channels to reap the related spillover effects of SEZs (Engman *et al.*, 2007).
4	Revenue contribution	SEZs are expected ensure a fair flow of revenue to the government through different sources, including revenue from rent and advances on open plots and Standard Design Factory (SDF)[ii], sale of water and electricity, and revenue through tax collections.
5	Spillover effects	These zones are expected to generate spillover effects for the domestic economy through purchase of domestic raw materials, capital goods and, outsourcing part of the production process in the DTA.

Source: Author's compilation based on various sources.

Note: i   In the case of all new upcoming SEZs, developers are either the government, or private, foreign or joint ventures.

       ii   If it is government SEZs, such revenue through rents and advances on open plots and SDF will be part of the government exchequer or otherwise, will be part of the private developer.

Initial economic conditions of the economy and location choice

If an economy had been completely insulated against the external world till embarking on such an experiment, then the creation and promotion of such zones could have a very little adverse impact on the fiscal position of the economy. Initially, the government has to incur a huge capital expenditure for providing a more conducive environment and institutional arrangements but, at the same time, if it succeeds in attracting fresh domestic and foreign investment, then it could contribute to various sources of government revenue in addition to ensuring alternative employment opportunities and livelihood to many.

China is a good example in this respect.[5] Thus, when the SEZ policy

---

5   Please see chapter 3 for detailed explanation on economic condition of China before introducing SEZ policy and kind of intervention taken through the SEZ policy.

was introduced in China, it created an additional source of government revenue. Moreover, both private and foreign investors participated in several infrastructure projects initiated by the Chinese government and helped reduce the capital expenditure outlay of the government. On the contrary, if SEZs were introduced after initiating the reform process, there could be possibilities of their depleting the revenue sources of the government. This is because, on account of a wider reform process implemented in the economy, the SEZ scheme would have hardly provided any special privileges to the investors, other than incentives. Further, the concentration of SEZs in a particular region might have exhausted the existing resource base and infrastructure facilities. This, in the long term, may further increase the fiscal responsibilities of the government.

Fiscal code and sectoral composition

In an attempt to popularize the SEZ scheme, the government comes up with a number of fiscal incentives in terms of tax concessions and/or subsidies that, in the present context, are referred to as the 'fiscal code'. The type of fiscal code extended to these zones also determines its possible repercussions on the fiscal position. Under the SEZs scheme, if the government offers preferential tariff rates in place of quantitative restrictions applicable elsewhere in the economy, there is a possibility of it contributing to the government's revenue pool. On the contrary, if it provides a reduced tariff structure and/or gives exemption from domestic taxes, in such a situation it can have a revenue depletion effect. At the same time, the sectoral choice and composition of SEZs also can influence the government's revenue state. For instance, the government may incur a very light fiscal burden if it chooses sectors that require very low imports, but can command a higher international demand and export earnings. On the contrary, if SEZs are promoted in sectors that exhibit a high import intensity of high-value products, then it would definitely lead to a substantial revenue loss to the government.

The approach

In the present context, the fiscal implications of SEZs for the economy as a whole are analysed within a resource cost framework. The analysis is based on aggregated data related to the seven conventional SEZs of the country (Kandla, Santacruz, Noida, Chennai, Cochin, Falta and Vizag SEZs) collected from the respective development commissioners' offices. The reference period spans 1990–91 to 2007–08.[6] The data on costs include the total government expenditure incurred in respect of each zone over the years for maintaining the administrative machinery (revenue expenditure), development and maintenance costs (capital expenditure) and the revenue foregone under the central excise and custom duties.[7] The various other components of revenue loss to the government have not been considered due to data-specific problems involved in dealing with the resource cost incurred by each SEZ. In fact, the problem associated with collecting information on the various costs involved in the promotion of such zones is not specific to Indian zones alone, a fact well acknowledged by various studies with reference to other countries as well.[8] On the benefit side, we have considered data only on NFE and the revenue earned from land rent and advances.

Given these constraints, the analysis has been restricted to only a few components of the resource cost and the direct impact of SEZs on the fiscal position of the economy that occur in the short term (indirect fiscal repercussions of SEZs in the long term are not considered). Thus, the revenue loss to the government exchequer and such other items that contribute significantly to an additional expenditure on the part of the government together determine the resource value that the government has to forego in order to earn a rupee in terms of NFE earnings[9] from these zones. The value is assumed to be between 0 and 1. This, in the present context, is used for comparing the real resource cost involved in generating NFE earnings over the reference period.[10] Before looking into the value of resource cost that

---

6 This is to be noted that, the resource cost analysis is restricted only to 1990–91, whereas individual components of resource costs are explained for the period 1986–87 to 2007–08.

7 Up to 1999–2000, revenue-foregone figure includes both central excise and custom duties, whereas, since 2000–01, it includes only custom duty.

8 For instances, see Warr (1988, 1989).

9 In order to identify resource costs involved in these zones, in the present exercise, we have not considered exports, but only high net foreign exchange earnings NFE. The objective of policymakers is not just export promotion, but also ensuring NFE. In the case of higher import values, a corresponding increase in exports may not generate welfare impact on the domestic economy. In such a case, export earnings get equalized with imports payments. Furthermore, based on the objectives of assessment, it can be modified accordingly and other proposed benefits can be employed in its analysis.

10 If, the scope of the study is extended to the disaggregate level, i.e., across zones, then a corresponding analysis will be helpful in ranking zones in terms of their relative efficiency.

the government has to forego to earn a rupee in terms of NFE earnings, it is necessary to compute a few basic estimates to assess the specific benefits in relation to specific components of resource costs involved in their promotion. They are as follows:

$$\text{R1}_{it} = r_{it} - re_{it} \tag{5.1}$$

It measures the partial net revenue earned by each zone. It is simply the difference between revenue earned (through rent and advance) and revenue expenditure incurred by each zone over the years. This helps us understand whether each zone has managed to generate resources needed for covering at least its administrative costs if not profits. A positive value indicates a light burden on the central government for its administration:

$$\text{R2}_{it} = r_{it} - (re_t + ce_t) \tag{5.2}$$

It measures the total net revenue earned in each zone. It is derived by taking the difference between the revenue earned (on rent and advances) and the total (revenue and capital) expenditure incurred by each zone over the years. This reveals whether each zone is capable of generating the resources needed for administrative maintenance and various zonal development projects. A positive value indicates less burden on the central government in maintaining administration and development of a zone.[11]

$$\text{RC1}_t = \Sigma Rf_t / \text{NFE}_t \tag{5.3}$$

The above equation estimates the value of resource cost involved in generating a unit of foreign exchange earnings; it is a partial estimation of resource cost as it considers only the revenue forgone as the total cost in its numerator, whereas the government also incurs a very huge amount in the form of revenue and capital expenditure.[12] Thus, Equation (5.3) could be

---

11 Results corresponding to Equations (5.1) and (5.2) need to be intrepreted very carefully. In the present case, developer of SEZs is the central government. Thus, the corresponding values outline the fiscal implication of SEZs for the government. On the other hand, if developers are private and/or joint venture, then the corresponding revenues are collected and owned by such entities and also the required capital expenditure is borne by developers. In the case of revenue expenditure, though officials (custom and excise officers) are appointed by the government, the respective developers are expected to pay the government salary and other allowances of such officers over and above the actual. Thus, in this case too revenue expenditure falls under respective developers.

12 This depends on the ownership pattern of SEZs. As seven SEZs covered in the present analysis are centrally owned, the government has to bear both revenue and capital expenditure.

extended to examine revenue and expenditure of the fiscal implications of SEZs. It can be considered as the total resource cost (RC2) incurred by the government in earning a rupee of foreign exchange from these zones.

$$RC2_t = \sum Rf_t + e_t / NFE_t \qquad (5.4)$$

Connotations used in Equations (5.1)–(5.4) represent the following: R1 represents partial net revenue earned, t stands for time period under consideration; i indicates zone under consideration, r revenue earned on rent and advance, re stands for administrative (revenue) expenditure incurred towards maintenance of a separate administration wing in each zone, R2 represents the total revenue earned, ce represents the capital expenditure incurred, RC1 represents partial resource costs, Rf stands for revenue foregone under customs and central excise duties exemptions, NFE denotes net foreign exchange earnings, RC2 represents the total resource costs, and e stands for additional expenditure incurred in playing the role of a facilitator of SEZs. This includes revenue and capital expenditures of the government.

Results and discussion

The seven zones taken up for discussion in the present case are owned by the central government, which also assumes the role of a developer. In order to develop plots and provide better infrastructure facilities within each zone, the government envisaged an outlay of ₹ 673.39 crore for the period 1986–87 to 2007–08. This could amount to a much higher figure if we consider the capital expenditure incurred by the government for each zone since inception. The registration of an upward trend in the capital outlay, particularly during the current SEZ period, reflecting the serious efforts on the part of the government towards improving the infrastructure facilities in these zones (Figure 5.1). Besides capital expenditure, the government has incurred a total expenditure of ₹ 303.63 crore over the last 22 years for the maintenance of separate administrative wings in these seven zones. Unlike capital expenditure, in respect of this expenditure no specific trend is observed because, the outlay on this front is guided by the recommendations of the Pay Commission, not by any specific industrial or trade policy (Figure 5.2).

Figure 5.1: Trends in the Total Capital Expenditure of the Select SEZs

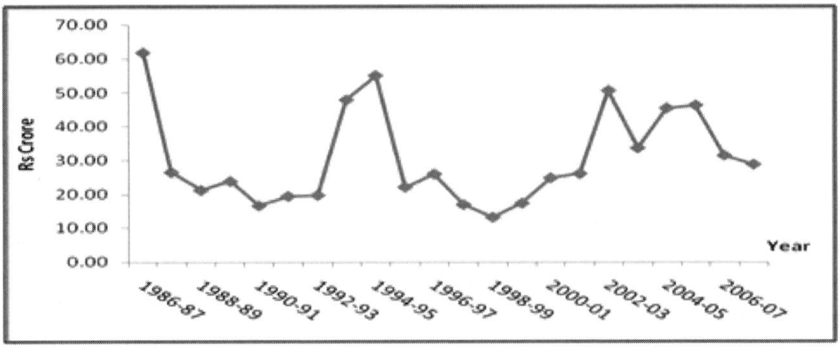

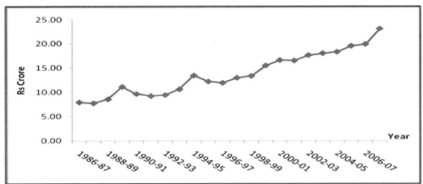

Source: Based on data collected from the seven conventional SEZs' development commissioner offices.

Note: Values are in ₹ crore and at constant price (1999–2000).

Figure 5.2: Trends in the Total Revenue Expenditure of the Select SEZs

Source: Based on data collected from the seven conventional SEZs' development commissioner offices.

Note: Values are in ₹ crore and at constant price (1999–2000).

Revenue and capital expenditure of investment undertaken so far amounts to ₹ 977.02 crore in respect of these seven zones (Figure 5.3). It is to be noted here that in the present analysis, we have not considered the government investment till 1980 and the inclusion of such outlay would have inflated the corresponding capital outlay and the government's total budgetary outlay for these zones.

Figure 5.3: Trends in the Total Budgetary Outlay for the Select SEZs
(Revenue and capital expenditure)

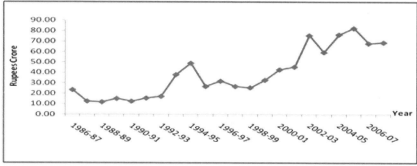

Source: Based on data collected from the seven conventional SEZs' development commissioner offices.

Note: Values are in ₹ crore and at constant prices (1999–2000).

The revenue foregone by the government exchequer (through customs and central excise exemptions) since 1990–91, from the seven zones amounts to ₹ 20,634.19 crore. The extent of revenue varies across over the years. The steep decline in the late 1990s could be attributed to a slowdown in demand for imports from these zones in view of the East Asian Crisis. Again, in the current SEZ phase, a marginal fall in the revenue foregone for the period between 2002–03 and 2005–06 and an upward trend thereafter is noticed.

As against the total government revenue and capital expenditure to the tune of ₹ 303.03 and ₹ 673.90 crore, respectively, these zones have cumulatively earned a revenue of ₹ 414.40 crore (Figure 5.5).[13] Figure 5.6 shows a steep increase in NFE from the seven conventional SEZs in the current phase. In this context, a look at the net revenue earned by these zones provides interesting insights. Partial net revenue earnings, as measured through R1 (as specified in equation 5.1) show a steady increase over the years, particularly during the SEZs period (Figure 5.7). This could be attributed to a steep increase in the number of exporting units in these seven conventional SEZs during the current period *vis-á-vis* EPZ period. This steady increase is a positive development in that these zones have managed to earn enough revenue to meet at least the administration costs, if not profits However, looking at

---

13 Due to data limitations, in this study, we have computed the total revenues from rent and advances. It does not include revenue from sale of water, electricity, etc.

the phenomenon through R2 gives a negative picture, that is, a continuous net revenue loss to the government (Figure 5.8). However, one may argue that increased revenue earning is not the main concern (of the government) underlying its SEZ policy. Therefore, the inference that SEZs can be a drain on the government exchequer and that hardly any benefit accrues from them stands challenged. For this purpose, one has to take into account benefits accrued in the form of NFE earnings and costs associated with such benefits, since they constitute the prime objectives behind the promotion of EPZs/ SEZs in the country.

Figure 5.4: Trends in the Total Revenue Foregone under Custom and Central Excise Duties of the Selected SEZ

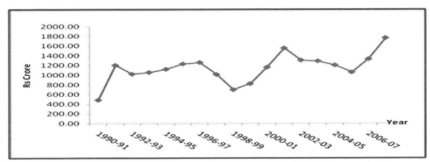

Source: Based on data collected from the seven conventional SEZs' development commissioner offices.

Note: Values are in ₹ crore and at constant prices (1999–2000).

Figure 5.5: Trends in the Total Rental Revenue Earned of Selected Seven SEZs

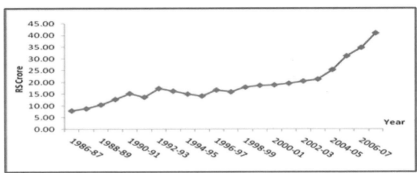

Source: Based on data collected from the seven conventional SEZs' development commissioner offices.

Note: Values are in ₹ crore and at constant prices (1999–2000).

Figure 5.6: Trends in Net Foreign Exchange Earnings of Selected Conventional SEZs

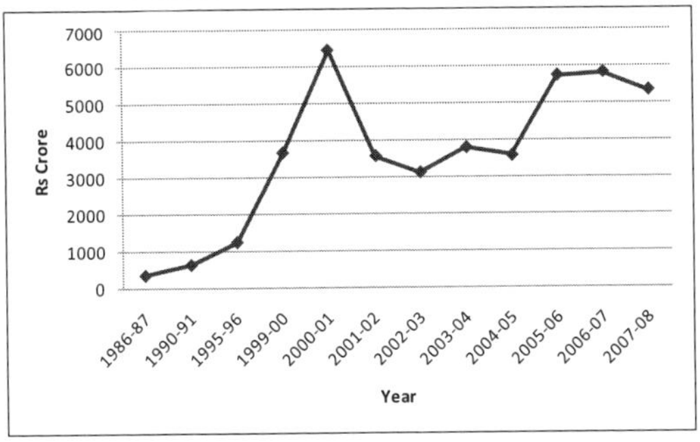

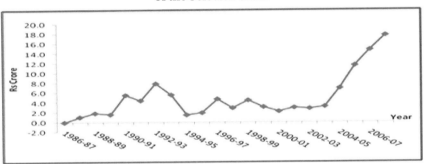

Source: Based on data collected from the seven conventional SEZs' development commissioner offices.

Note: Values are in ₹ crore and at constant prices (obtained after deflating from GDP (1999–2000).

Figure 5.7: Trends in the Partial Net Revenue Earned (R1) of the Selected SEZs

Source: Based on data collected from the seven conventional SEZs' development commissioner offices.

Note: Values are in ₹ crore and at constant price of 1999–2000.

To quantify the extent of revenue foregone for promoting each rupee of the net foreign exchange earned by these zones, partial and total resource cost as specified in equations 5.3 and 5.4 are estimated, respectively. The value of RC depends on two factors: (a) the net foreign exchange earnings; and (b) the value of total costs including both revenue foregone and expenditure incurred by the government.

If higher the total costs and lower the net foreign exchange earnings, then higher will be the corresponding RC. However, if the net foreign exchange

**Figure 5.8: Trends in the Total Net Revenue Earned (R2)
of the Selected SEZs**

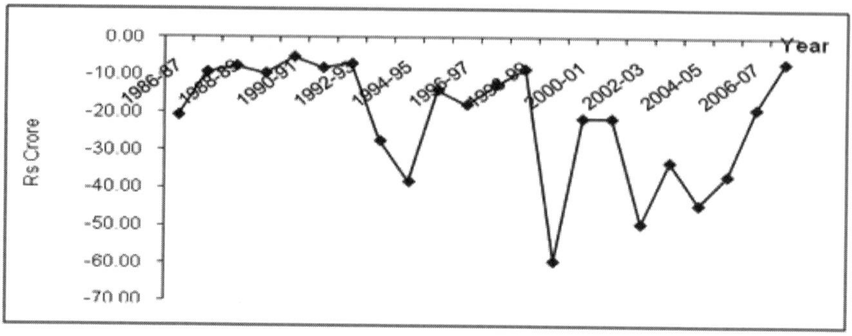

Source: Based on data collected from the seven conventional SEZs' development commissioner offices.

Note: Values are in ₹ crore and at constant prices (1999–2000).

earnings are much higher than the total costs incurred by the government, then the RC value will be lower. Lower the value, lower the RCs; however, higher values question the financial viability of SEZs. Partial resource cost as specified in equation 5.3 indicates that in order to promote each rupee of NFE, the government incurred a resource cost to the tune of ₹ 0.30 for 2007–08 (Figure 5.9), though with fluctuations over the years. This indicates that in real terms, in order to promote one rupee of NFE, the government incurred RCs to the tune of ₹ 0.30 (in the case of RC1), whereas with only ₹ 0.70 NFE actually added to the government exchequer.

In fact, for the first two years of the 1990s (1991–92 and 1992–93), the associated resource cost is found quite higher than per unit NFE earnings. Thereafter, it shows a continuous declining trend. This high resource cost in the early 1990s could be attributed to a slowdown in the export earnings due to the disintegration of the USSR, which was, however, not accompanied by an immediate and equal drop in the import payment and hence a low NFE, but a substantial revenue loss to the government under the head of customs tax. Moreover, a substantial reduction in RC1 values over the period, among others, could be due to a gradual reduction in import tariffs since the early 1990s. However, a slight upward trend noticed for the initial few years of 2000s (current SEZs period) could be due to an increase in the number of exporting units, and subsequently increase in the demand for imports. More or less similar trend is noticed with respect to RC2 (Figure 5.10).

Figure 5.9: Trends in the Partial Resource Cost (RC1) of Selected SEZs

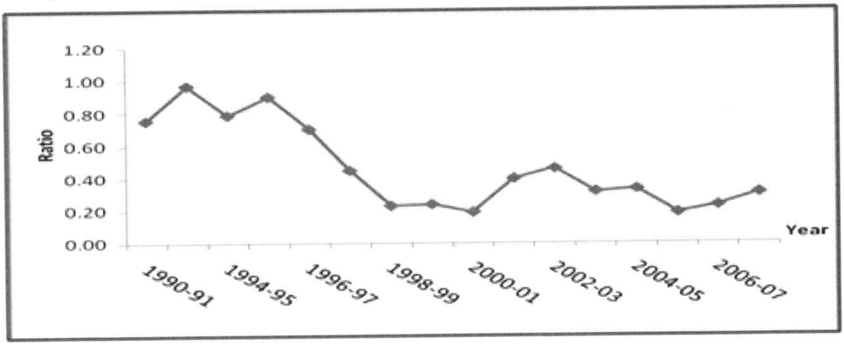

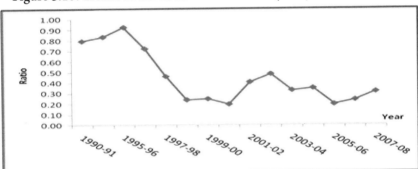

Source: Respective SEZ development commissioner offices.

Figure 5.10: Trends in the Total Resource Cost (RC2) of Selected SEZs

Source: Respective SEZ development commissioner office.

Summary

Apart from outlining SEZs' contribution to trade expansion, it is equally important to explain the fiscal implications associated with the promotion of SEZs for the economy as a whole, especially considering their known impact on distribution dimensions. Our analysis, based on a 'resource cost' framework (using the data collected from seven conventional SEZs and taking 1990–91 to 2007–08 as the reference period) reveals that the government has spent huge sums as part of its role as a facilitator, besides foregoing a substantial revenue. However, what the computations carried out by the study indicate can be considered as an underestimate of the actual net costs involved in the promotion of SEZs. Perhaps, the corresponding ratio of revenue foregone to generate each rupee of NFE earnings, may point to a higher value if one were to consider all other sources of revenue foregone by both the central and state governments. For instance, as per the Union Budget 2012, the amount of revenue foregone for 2011–12 amounts to ₹ 4,560 crore as against ₹ 2,324 crore for 2009–10, raising a serious question thereby about the financial viability of SEZs in the country.

Proponents of SEZs may claim that SEZs expansion will lead to an increase in the export value, better employment opportunities and increased investment, which by themselves are capable of generating spillover effects for the domestic economy. But the scepticism that, in the process, it may adversely affect the distributional aspect of the economy cannot be ignored. Largely so given their nature of diverting resources towards the SEZs' expansion and accompanied by a substantial revenue loss to both the central and state governments. Moreover, there is an absolute paucity of data in the public domain to undertake any rigorous analysis with regard to the fiscal viability of SEZs. Given the importance of ascertaining the costs involved in generating each rupee of exports and NFE through promotion of SEZs as also, from the point of view of the country's economic accounting, it is incumbent on the government to devise appropriate policy interventions to record such activities within the sphere of SEZs for quantifying such costs that hold significant fiscal implications for the economy as a whole.

6

Special Economic Zones and the Question of Efficiency[1]

Background

Ensuring efficiency in the production process of economic units is indisputably an essential component and goal of the policy. In the case of SEZs, the efficiency issues assume greater prominence considering the special attention extended to these enclaves in terms of liberalized trade, fiscal and administrative system relative to other segments of the economic system, which in turn, set a benchmark for performance standards, and more so because, these are considered the engines of growth in the trade sector. However, the literature available on the performance analysis of these enclaves based on aggregate indicators tends to overlook the possibilities that, while the performance of these enclaves might have improved in absolute terms, they might have failed in meeting the objective of improving efficiency in production processes. The failure to understand the same may result in overrating the performance of enclaves in terms of utilization of their production capacity with little scope for further improvements in their role as engines of economic growth.

To probe this issue further, let us consider the following scenario (Figure 6.1a) in which exports from these enclaves have increased almost at double digits in the year t_1 (point B), as against its value in the year t (point A). This, however, does not show the corresponding increase in the exports value as the most optimum possible output, given the input mix and a special policy-based provisions exclusively available to these zones. To state otherwise, are

---

1 Originally published in *Journal of Economic Policy Reform*, Vol. 15, Issue 4: 321–337, www.tandfonline.com/http://www.tandfonline.com/doi/full/10.1080/17487870.20 12.696420. However, substantial changes have been made.

these enclaves within the production possibility frontier (PPF) or are they at their optimum level? This scenario indicates the possibility that the figures shown to prove a substantial improvement in the performance of these enclaves might still be below the most efficient level of output. This also leaves us clueless as to whether the increase in the value of exports over the period is mainly due to a better utilization of the input mix by the existing exporting units or due to a mere increase in the number of exporting units and operational SEZs in the country or a rise in inflation. This increase in the number of exporting units and operational SEZs in the country in itself is questionable, given the apprehension that it merely amounts to a realignment of investment from domestic trade zone to SEZs. Thus, these alarming possibilities indicate that SEZs, perhaps, have not contributed much towards an overall improvement in the production capacity or efficiency of the economy, but have only brought about a realignment of investment.

Figure 6.1a: Optimum Export Value of SEZs over the Years – A Hypothetical Scenario

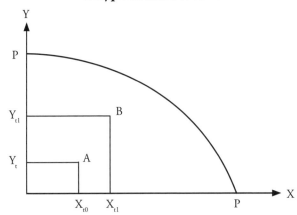

Source: Author's work.

Studies analysing the performance of these enclaves at the disaggregate levels rank them on the basis of their contribution to the total SEZ exports, NFE, employment, and investment. However, these studies concentrate solely on the relative performance of a given *vis-à-vis* others, while ignoring the possibility of discrepancies between a higher exporting zone and an efficient zone. For instance, a zone may be the highest exporter relative to other zones, but it may not be efficient in the production process, i.e., it might be far below the most optimum production level (point C in Figure

1b). However, a zone might show a low level of exports in relation to other zones, but might be making an optimum utilization of the input mix, that is, either it is on the PPF or very near the optimum production level, thereby indicating a very low level of inefficiency as compared to the other zone (point D in Figure 1c). If this scenario is indeed a plausible one, then it becomes necessary to carry out a performance comparison of zones based on the efficiency criterion as against the conventional practice of comparing their aggregate indicators, and subsequently to explain the factors that contribute to variations in efficiency scores across zones and also to probe whether, over the years, there has been a convergence or divergence of efficiency across zones. In the light of these factors, it becomes imperative to analyse the issue of efficiency, apart from delineating the trends and patterns in the trade performance of these enclaves, and also to investigate factors affecting efficiency scores of these enclaves.

**Figure 6.1b: A Comparison of Optimum Exports across Zones –
A Hypothetical Scenario**

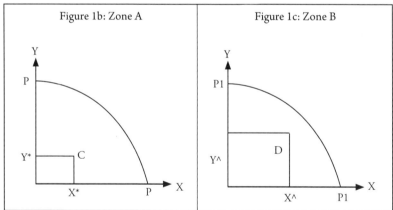

Source: Author's work.

Estimating efficiency – framework for analysis

A stochastic production function is employed in the present analysis for evaluating the efficiency of zones by constructing a frontier for SEZs at the national level, using individual zones as production units. Although different zones may be producing different products, it is common practice to construct a uniform frontier for the manufacturing sector as a whole.[2]

---

2   For instance, earlier studies, while estimating the efficiency of the Indian manufacturing

However, what we need to note in the case of these enclaves is that they are a privileged group of industrial ventures brought together for the promotion of exports. Thus, analysing firm-specific efficiency may not reveal the level of efficiency of each zone and the SEZ policy *per se*.

The production function we have used in the present analysis is a modified formulation of the standard production function. Conventional theory defines production as follows:

$$\text{Output} = f(\text{labour, raw material, capital stock}) \qquad (6.1)$$

Here, both output and inputs are measured in terms of market prices. In the case of SEZs, there is no such thing as output, as exports are considered as the total (effective) output. The very rationale underlying SEZs is that, the entire output produced by them is meant to be exported. Thus, the first assumption is that all exports generated by SEZs amounts to the gross value of output. On the input side, we have considered the total number of labourers employed in each zone over the years and the import of raw material and capital goods for each year. Thus, in the context of SEZs, the efficiency of a given zone refers to its capability to produce the maximum possible output (real exports), utilizing the existing liberalized import regime alongside a supportive mechanism provided by the policy. Thus, one can envisage a scenarios where a zone that is not in the forefront in terms of higher export earnings relative to other zones may be producing an optimum output (exports), given the supportive mechanism available to it. Similarly, a zone, while accounting for the highest export earnings *vis-à-vis* others, may still be below its optimum production capacity. Thus, there could be a mismatch between the export performance of a given zone and its efficiency score. In view of a small number of observations, the available data does not permit the use of a translog production function, known for its flexibility; hence, we have employed Cobb–Douglas Production Function[3] following the argument of

---

sector, have considered it as a production unit and did not consider variations within a manufacturing sector at the subsector level.

3   An alternative tool for efficiency estimation is non-parametric programming approach. However, there are a number of limitations associated with this technique. For instance, (a) it is an extreme point technique, noise such as measurement error can cause significant problems; (b) though this technique can show how well an economic unit is doing compared to others, the results obtained through it cannot be compared with a theoretical maximum; and (c) because it is a non-parametric technique, statistical hypothesis tests are difficult to carry out. Thus, given these limitations, the

Madalla (1979) that TE measurement is quite insensitive to the functional form of a production frontier. The estimable form of the model is as follows:

$$Ln(X_{it}) = \alpha + \beta_1 \ln L_{it} + \beta_2 \ln R_{it} + \beta_3 \ln CG_{it} + v_{it} + \mu_{it} \qquad (6.2)$$

To identify the determinants of inefficiency, we have adopted the procedure developed by Battese and Coelli (1995). The model specification is

$$\mu_{it} = \delta_0 + \delta_1 \ln AZ_{it} + \delta_2 \ln DU_{it} + \delta_3 \ln Gi_{it} + \delta_4 \text{PolicyDummy} + W_{it} \qquad (6.3)$$

In this model, X represents the value (at constant prices) of exports of a zone i in the year t; RM represents the value of raw material imports (value at constant prices) of a zone i in the year t; L stands for the total labour employed in a zone i in the year t; CG denotes capital goods imports of a zone i in the year t; V_{it} are random variables, assumed to be independently and identically distributed (IID) with $N(0,\sigma u^2)$; W_{it} are non-negative random variables assumed to account for export inefficiency and are also assumed to be independently distributed with mean zero and variance σu^2; AZ_{it} is the total area of a zone i in the year t; DU_{it} denotes the concentration of units in a zone i in the year t (the ratio of exporting units to the area of a zone, capturing the clustering of units); Gi_{it} is government investment in a zone i in the year t; policy dummy [dummy variable (0 = for EPZs period and 1 for SEZs period] is used to capture policy changes occurring in the year 2000–01; $i = 1, 2, \ldots,$ 7 refers to zone and $t = 1985$–86, 1986–87, 2007–08 is the time period under consideration; ln denotes natural logarithm.

With respect to coverage, the present exercise is restricted to SEZs that have been operating prior to the introduction of the SEZ policy.[4]

Accordingly, we have selected the following seven conventional SEZs: Kandla (KSEZ), Santacruz (SSEZ), Noida (NSEZ), Chennai (MSEZ), Cochin (CSEZ), Falta (FSEZ), and Vizag (VSEZ). The reference period of the study spread over 1986–87 to 2007–08[5] with the related data obtained from the development commissioner office of the respective SEZs. Of the

present analysis is restricted to the stochastic frontier production function approach and more specifically Cobb–Douglas production function, for its simplicity and logarithmic nature of analysis.

4   With this criterion, the selected seven SEZs represent an entire population, because there were only seven fully functional SEZs in the country before the introduction of the SEZ policy.

5   There is no published data source available in the public domain regarding various issues pertaining to SEZ expansion in the country. Thus, we have had to restrict our analysis to 2007–08 based on data collected as part of the author's fieldwork carried out in these seven zones.

seven zones, Vizag SEZ setup in 1989–90, became operational in 1994. Therefore, the data set for Vizag is available from 1995 to 1996 onwards. Also, data for some of the variables was not available for some periods. Thus, the available data represents an unbalanced panel of seven zones for a period of 22 years (the total number of observations being 123).

One of the conventional methods used in assessing the efficiency of a production unit is to estimate labour productivity – the ratio of output to the total number of labourers. Before estimating TE through a stochastic production frontier, we have estimated the labour productivity of these enclaves which ranges from 0.04 crore rupees to 0.15 crore rupees over the last 22 years (Figure 7.2) with a significant increase over the years, specifically during the SEZ period. For the latest available year, the labour productivity of Vizag SEZ is the highest followed by Cochin (Figure 6.3). However, over the years, we have noticed substantial fluctuations.

Figure 6.2: Average Labour Productivity of SEZs over the Years

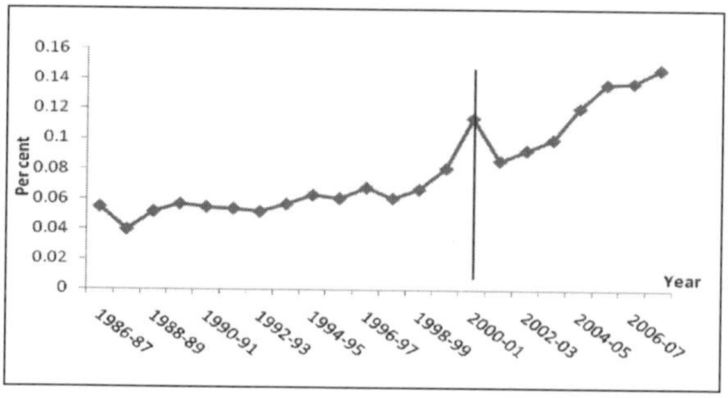

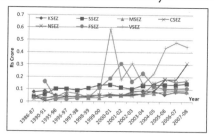

Source: Based on data collected from the seven conventional SEZs' development commissioner offices.
Note: Values are in ₹ crore.

Figure 6.3: Trends in Labour Productivity of SEZs across Zones

Source: Based on data collected from the seven conventional SEZs' development commissioner offices.
Note: Values are in ₹ crore.

An analysis of the average labour productivity, covering both EPZ (1986–87 to 1999–2000), the current SEZ periods (2000–01 to 2007–08) and also for the entire reference period indicates that (Table 6.1), while, on an average, the introduction of the SEZ policy in place of the conventional EPZ structure of the country has had a significant and positive impact on the labour productivity scores of SEZs, the labour productivity of SEZs continues to remains quite low, calling for some corrective measures to tackle this issue. Although the evaluation of labour productivity throws some light on the performance level of an economic unit, in this case the SEZs, it seems only a partial picture. Therefore, it is quite necessary to have an integrated approach, factoring in all the major input variable of the production function in relation to output in assessing efficiency. This is taken up for discussion in the subsequent subsections.

Table 6.1: Average Labour Productivity of SEZs under Major Policy Regimes

	KSEZ	SEEPZ	MSEZ	CSEZ	NSEZ	FSEZ	VSEZ	All SEZs
1986–87 to 2007–08	0.055	0.083	0.037	0.028	0.036	0.077	NA	0.059
1986–87 to 1999–00	0.070	0.131	0.068	0.124	0.108	0.167	0.350	0.117
2000–01 to 2007–08	0.060	0.101	0.048	0.063	0.062	0.110	0.289	0.080

Source: Based on data collected from the seven conventional SEZs' development commissioner offices.
Note: Values are in ₹ crore and at constant value.

Results and discussion

An aggregate efficiency scenario

The average TE of SEZs, over the reference period, ranges from 0.31 to 0.75 per cent, whereas the average efficiency score of the total selected SEZs for the entire reference period is found to be 0.53 per cent (Table 6.3 and Figure 6.4). This suggests that, on an average, SEZs are 53 per cent efficient in terms of optimally producing exports with a given input mix, as against to the best managed SEZs. What it implies is that, on an average, it is possible to improve the efficiency of SEZs by 47 per cent with a given mix of inputs. This, however, raises a broader question about efficiency with which the resources in these enclaves are being utilized towards meetings their objectives. As Hill and Kalirajan (1993) argue, a plant or an industrial unit can be considered technically efficient if its TE score is not less than 75 per cent. If we analyse the technical efficiency of SEZs within this framework, one can observe that these enclaves are highly inefficient at the aggregate level.

Figure 6.4: Average Technical Efficiency Scores of Selected SEZs

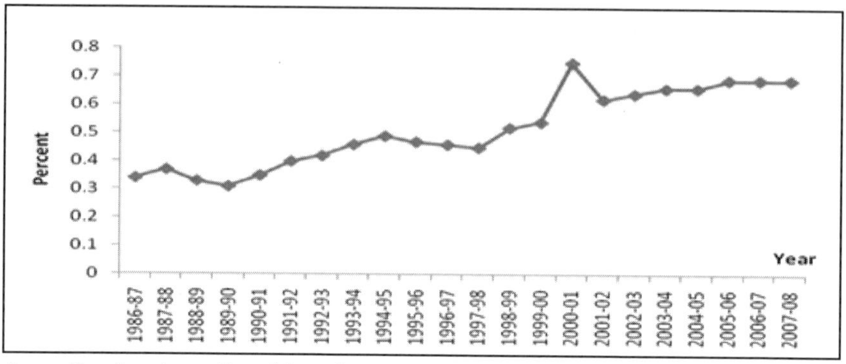

Source: Based on data collected from the seven conventional SEZs' development commissioner offices.

Note: Values are in ₹ crore and at constant value.

Changes in policy regime and efficiency scores

The average TE score for the EPZ period as a whole, that is, from 1986–87 to 1999–2000, is observed to below 0.50 per cent (Table 6.3), thereby indicating the sluggish structure of EPZ in terms of infusing efficiency in the performance of these enclaves. However, the TE scores during the SEZs period are observed to have increased substantially across all the zones, especially the average TE scores during this period reached to 0.67 per cent. This can also be interpreted as inefficiency being reduced substantially across the seven zones during the current SEZ regime. This corroborates the government initiatives under the SEZ policy, which have resulted not only in higher export earnings, but also improved efficiency scores of these enclaves. However, the improvement seems to have been temporary, for, the TE scores of these zones are again found below 75 per cent which, in the literature are considered as the 'threshold level' for measuring the technical efficiency or inefficiency of any economic unit. These observations warrant a further streamlining of the SEZ structure, taking into account the difficulties involved in the operational process, rather than just extending the liberal fiscal incentives.

Table 6.2: Trends in Technical Efficiency Scores of SEZs over the Period

	KSEZ	SSEZ	MSEZ	CSEZ	NSEZ	FSEZ	VSEZ
First phase of EPZ expansion							
1986–87	0.46	0.39	0.19	NA	0.31	NA	NA
1987–88	0.45	0.38	NA	NA	0.27	NA	NA
1988–89	0.48	0.41	0.32	0.16	0.30	NA	NA
1989–90	NA	0.45	0.30	0.20	0.35	0.23	NA
1990–91	0.55	NA	0.34	0.19	0.41	0.25	NA
Second phase of EPZ expansion							
1991–92	0.50	0.50	NA	0.26	0.40	0.34	NA
1992–93	0.45	0.56	0.41	NA	0.44	0.24	NA
1993–94	0.53	0.58	0.56	0.37	NA	0.28	NA
1994–95	0.54	0.62	0.49	0.34	0.48	NA	NA
1995–96	0.59	0.60	0.46	0.32	0.52	0.34	NA
1996–97	NA	0.67	0.47	0.39	0.51	0.27	NA
1997–98	0.60	NA	0.48	0.35	0.52	0.28	NA
1998–99	0.56	0.76	NA	0.37	0.55	0.36	NA
1999–2000	0.60	0.73	0.49	NA	0.61	0.54	0.26
SEZ regime							
2000–01	0.79	0.80	0.60	NA	0.71	0.78	0.81
2001–02	0.61	0.84	0.54	0.49	NA	0.82	0.42
2002–03	0.68	0.79	0.55	0.60	0.63	0.74	0.46
2003–04	0.69	0.83	0.56	0.60	0.72	0.86	0.36
2004–05	0.73	0.86	0.57	0.57	0.70	0.82	0.35
2005–06	0.74	0.87	0.73	0.63	0.74	0.62	0.46
2006–07	0.79	0.85	0.73	0.64	0.75	0.60	0.50
2007–08	0.78	0.87	0.67	0.63	0.76	0.61	0.52

Source: Based on data collected from the seven conventional SEZs' development commissioner offices.
Note: Values are in ₹ crore and at constant value.

Table 6.3: Average Technical Efficiency Scores of SEZs
under Major Policy Regimes

	KSEZ	SSEZ	MSEZ	CSEZ	NSEZ	FSEZ	VSEZ	All SEZs
1986–87 to 1999–2000	0.53	0.55	0.41	0.30	0.44	0.31	NA	0.42
2000–01 to 2007–08	0.73	0.84	0.62	0.59	0.72	0.73	0.49	0.67
1986–87 to 2007–08	0.61	0.67	0.50	0.42	0.53	0.50	0.46	0.53

Source: Based on data collected from the seven conventional SEZs' development commissioner offices.
Note: Values are in ₹ crore and at constant value.

Efficiency of SEZs at the disaggregate level

Among the selected SEZs, over the reference period (1986–87 to 2007–08), Santacruz SEZ is found to be the most efficient zone with an average TE score of 0.67 per cent. However, with a 0.42 per cent TE score, Cochin SEZ happens to be the least efficient zone (Table 6.3). During the EPZ period (1986–87 to 1999–2000), among the seven zones, Santacruz and Kandla SEZs have recorded better efficiency scores (0.55 and 0.53, respectively) as compared to other zones operating on the same frontier. However, during the current phase of SEZ expansion, the average TE score of Santacruz works out to be 0.84 per cent, implying thereby that among the seven zones, Santacruz SEZ has been relatively better off in terms of maintaining efficiency standard. This is followed by the TE scores of Kandla, Falta and Noida SEZs. It is to be noted that as far as the gross value of exports and the per unit value of exports is concerned, FSEZ ranks the lowest, whereas in respect of efficiency scores, it fares better than NSEZ, MSEZ, CSEZ and VSEZ. This reveals that there exists a contradiction in the ranking of zones based on export earnings and efficiency scores. What comes to the fore is the discrepancy between higher export earnings and optimum export earnings, raising in the process questions about the efficacy of the measurement tool currently used to evaluate these enclaves.

Undoubtedly, there exist significant variations in the TE scores across the zones, as well as years within zones. In this connection, the next question we need to address is whether there is a convergence or divergence of efficiency scores across the seven zones. That is to examine the possibility of there being no real change in the rankings of zones, and that the perceived change in rankings is merely due to a change in gap measured in terms of efficiency. Such a phenomenon can be observed when a low-performing zone exhibits a faster improvement than a better-performing zone, and in such a situation, one can notice a convergence of efficiency scores across the zones, whereas in an opposite scenario, it could lead to a divergence of the same. Such convergence analysis, in general, also helps us understand whether the dispersion of efficiency distribution would narrow over a period (Mukherjee and Ray, 2004 and 2005).[6]

An analysis of this issue based on Sigma convergence (Figure 6.5) indicates a convergence of efficiency scores across the zones over the years. At the same time, one can notice fluctuations in their scores over the years, specifically after the enactment of the SEZ policy in the country. The gap between better and poorly performing zones has been narrowing down, as observed over clearly in the last three years, that is, 2005–08.

Figure 6.5: Trends in Coefficient of Variations of Technical Efficiency Scores across SEZs over Time

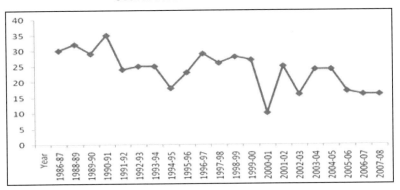

Source: Author's estimation.

Determinants of inefficiency scores

Besides holding significant policy implications, the determinants of inefficiency scores can help correct aberrations if any. The land area allocated to SEZs is one of the major issues being debated across the country that needs to be attended to in the first place. On an average, the SEZs in the analysis hold 100–1,000 ha of land. It is generally assumed that larger the area of

---

6 This aspect is explained through different techniques in the literature. The most widely applied techniques include Beta Convergence and Sigma Convergence (also known as coefficient of variation). In the present exercise, we have considered only seven zones and hence, difficult to measure convergence through Beta convergence technique.

land, higher will be the export efficiency of SEZs. This assumption has gained acceptance in our analysis, as the area spread of a zone exhibits a negative sign and is statistically significant with respect to inefficiency, thereby indicating that the converse of it has a positive relation with efficiency scores (Table 7.4). The concentration of units reveals both significant and negative signs with respect to technical inefficiency, indicating the presence of agglomeration/ clustering of export units within a zone that has significant impact in terms of improving the efficiency of a given zone. One can also infer that, unless accompanied by a clustering of export units, the area spread of SEZs may not be effective. Government investments, however, have turned negative but exhibit an insignificant relation with respect to technical inefficiency. This is quite contrary to our expectations. However, this offers an inconclusive inference with regard to government investments and efficiency of SEZs. All the same, this indicates that the government's efforts towards improving and providing world-class infrastructure within these zones have a positive influence in terms of shaping the efficiency estimation of these enclaves. It can be seen that the efficiency scores of SEZs have increased during the current SEZ period in line with the government's efforts towards increased investment on infrastructure, but this is not proved empirically, as it has not turned out to be statistically significant. Finally, the dummy variable capturing the impact of policy changes on the efficiency of these zones is found to be statistically significant, but with a negative sign with respect to technical inefficiency, thereby indicating that the government's efforts (in the form of policy measures) in terms of shifting the focus from conventional EPZs to SEZs have been quite useful not only in improving the trade performance but also encouraging an efficient use of resources in the production process with a view to generating an optimum level of output.

Table 6.4: Determinants of Export Inefficiency

Parameters	Estimated values
Constant	3.45 (5.15)*
Area of zone	-0.247 (-3.59*)
Clustering/Concentration of units	-1.5 (-4.42)*
Government investment	-0.064 (-1.258)

Parameters	Estimated values
Dummy	-0.27 (-3.12)*

Source: Author's estimation.
Note: Figures in parenthesis are t values; *refers to significance at 1 per cent level.

Summary

What follows from our analysis is that instead of following the conventional practice of evaluating the performance of SEZs based on aggregate performance indicators, it is imperative that we evaluate the policy and performance of these enclaves in terms of technical efficiency in the production process. This is because, the former approach, if employed may result in overrating the performance of these enclaves with little scope for further improvements in their role as engines of economic growth. Although theoretically it is possible for a zone to score better on the basis of increased exports as compared to other zones, practically it may turn out to be inefficient in the terms of optimally managing the production process. Keeping this critical aspect in view, the present analysis, carried out with respect to the seven conventional SEZs, indicates that the policy changes introduced in 2000–01 have had a significant impact on their output/export efficiency. At the same time, despite a steady improvement in the efficiency scores during the SEZ expansion, these enclaves are currently performing much below their potential. Of the seven conventional SEZs, the performance of Santacruz and Kandla SEZs has been relatively better than the other zones operating on the same production frontier (for the entire reference period). On the determinants side, besides policy intervention, large areas with a clustering of units are observed to have positively impacted the efficiency scores of these enclaves. Nevertheless, there is much scope for improving the efficiency standards of these enclaves by way of disciplining as well as revamping the structure of these SEZs. This could be better achieved by an in-depth analysis of the problems and prospects of each zone on a case-by-case basis, rather than following a one-size-fits-all policy being followed for all zones.

7

Conclusions

When it comes to evaluating an economic policy, three important elements need to be understood and examined carefully. First, the rationale underlying an economic policy, i.e., is there a clear understanding of why a particular policy is being put in place; do we have a clear idea of the expected benefits and associated negative impacts of a given policy; do we know the presence and experience of similar policies, if any, in other countries as well – have they been successful venture or flawed attempts and what factors underlies the outcome of such policies? Second, it is necessary to investigate how a policy is being implemented. Because, a policy may fulfil the first order condition, i.e., clarity underlying a policy but there can be flaws at the implementation. This is specifically so, because a policy is framed by the government[1] but it is bureaucracy that implements the policy at different levels. Thus, the coordination or conflict between these two actors involved in the formulation and execution of a policy, respectively, does help to explain the third-order condition, i.e., evaluating a policy document, namely, performance. However, studies evaluating of a policy document largely concentrate on the performance aspect based on a few selected indicators without attempting to accommodate the underlying rationale and implementation part of it which actually influence the outcome of it, that is, a policy document is mostly evaluated on the basis of symptoms rather than the causal factors. An in-depth analysis of India's current policy on special economic zones within this framework helps us argue that SEZ policy in India has partially failed to meet the first-order condition, that is, the logic underlying the promotion of SEZs. In fact, policymakers have modelled India's policy on

---

1   It can be either central government and/or state-/provincial-level government.

SEZs after China's model without giving a thought to the flaws inherent in China's SEZs policy. Further, it is important to note that the success of SEZs in China need not necessarily be attributed to China's 'SEZ policy' *per se*; rather various supportive mechanisms, both internal and external, are found to have played an important role in scripting this success story, thus indicating that SEZs cannot be expected to deliver an optimum performance under *ceteris paribus* condition; rather it requires a careful identification and execution of supportive factors, which may vary across countries, SEZs and/or between sectors within a given economy. Moreover, Chinese SEZs are not as green as hypothesized and claimed by Indian policymakers. In fact, the promotion of SEZs has resulted in distortions within China's economy. In fact, India's SEZs make a clear departure from those of China. However, the adoption of the China's model of trade policy by the country appears as an improvement over the conventional EPZs. Thereby, it fulfils its promise of promoting qualitative transformation of EPZs. Yet, despite numerous credits in its favour, the SEZ policy in India needs a pragmatic revisit. Specifically, the current SEZ policy also seems to be suffering from certain flaws at the implementation level. The most important argument in this respect relates to the various flaws inherent in the policy, which are in conflict with the other development-related objectives of the economy. The major ones include the government's stand on incentives offered to different actors involved in the process, land acquisition, and compensation formulae and the sectoral and geographical expansion of SEZs in the country. Thus, as a way ahead, we argue that there is an increasing need for restructuring the SEZ scheme in the country specifically in terms of identifying the problems and prospects associated with the expansion of SEZs rather than just extending liberal incentive schemes. With regard to the performance of these special enclaves, certain ambiguous inferences emerge. Although in absolute terms their performance seems quite promising, it has not proved to be quite effective in diversifying the country's export basket and promoting a strong industrial base. Further, there is hardly any evidence to the effect that they are playing an important role in employment generation and investment accumulation in the economy. In addition to this, the trade performance itself is questionable on the ground of fiscal viability of SEZs project and efficiency in the production process. As our analysis, based on a 'resource cost' framework, reveals, the government spends huge sums as part of its role as a facilitator, besides foregoing a substantial portion of revenue in the form of incentives to SEZs. However, what the computations carried out by the study indicate can be considered as an underestimation of the actual net costs involved in the promotion of SEZs. Perhaps, the corresponding ratio of revenue foregone in generating each rupee of NFE earning, may point to a higher value, if one were to consider all other revenue foregone from different sources by both the central and state government raising thereby a serious question about the financial viability of SEZs in the country. An analysis of the efficiency aspect of SEZs helps us argue that the conventional practice of evaluating the performance of SEZs based on the aggregate performance indicators may result in over-rating the performance of these enclaves with little scope for further improvements in their role as engines of economic growth. Although theoretically it is possible for a zone to score better on the basis of increased exports as compared to other zones, practically it may turn out to be inefficient in terms of optimally managing the production process. Keeping this critical aspect in view, the present analysis, carried out with respect to seven conventional SEZs, indicates that the policy changes introduced in 2000–01 have had a significant impact on their output/export efficiency. At the same time, despite a steady improvement in the efficiency scores during the SEZ expansion, these enclaves are currently performing much below their potential.

Based on an analysis of various policy documents we argue for a policy revision on the following ground: within a decade and half of the introduction of the SEZs policy in the country, the number of working SEZs has risen to 199, whereas 436 SEZs have been formally approved and 347 SEZs notified.[2] As opposed to this, China has created only five SEZs over the last three decades, based on the experience of a few initial SEZs. On the other hand, in India, most of the SEZ proposals have been approved by the Board of Approval (BoA). This is quite inconsistent with the practice followed in the country during EPZs regime with the government deliberating meticulously before taking decisions on the establishment new EPZs. Thus, very few EPZs were approved, while keeping in view the locational feasibility and sectoral composition of zones. However, the government seems to have abandoned the earlier cautious approach as can be seen from the present practice of notifying SEZs projects with no thought given to the probability of their success, locational advantages/disadvantages, availability of manpower etc.

---

2   As on 9 September 2015 (www.sezindia.nic.in) and excerpted on 14 April 2015.

in a given region. Furthermore, very little is made known about the problems and prospects of the newly notified SEZs. Coming up with dossiers with respect to each and every zone can be helpful in revisiting the existing EPZ policy as part of course correction and modification. The need to introduce an upper limit on the number of SEZs to be set up in the country also becomes important in view of a substantial revenue that the government may forego in respect of each zone with severe fiscal repercussions on the economy (at least in the short term), as explored by the current study.

Besides, SEZs receive preferential treatment in terms of privileges, which are not available to the rest of the economy. As a result, regions with SEZs receive more than their natural share of government resources at the cost of the development of other regions. This, in the long run, may result in regional disparities not only between SEZ and non-SEZ areas but also between rural and urban areas. Thus, a proper locational choice is essential to arrest disparities in development. This apart, the government should also make suitable interventions to prevent the concentration of SEZs in a few states, within a given state, and a few regions because, in the long run, this could not only widen the existing gaps between the developed and underdeveloped states but also could result in congestion, diseconomies of scale, etc.

As against the current trend of promoting SEZs in IT/ITes, where there is no sufficient scope for creating employment among unskilled workers, policymakers should focus on promoting SEZs in those industries in which India enjoys comparative advantage and has the potential to generate more employment and production network value chains. This approach can help tackle the problems related to regional disparities in development and thereby mitigate problems relating to migration. In this respect, the respective states may think of promoting SEZs in those sectors considered priority sectors for national development, while keeping in view each regions comparative advantage. Any such exercise can not only help increase India's share in the world market but also encourage traditional craftsmanship and employment generation. Diversification of the export basket can also be helpful in withstanding different types of external shocks besides boosting the performance of these zones. These corrective policy measures hinge on the question as to which type of land should be allowed for the expansion of SEZs. If every state could promote SEZs in those areas in which the state has a clear comparative advantage with regard to natural resources, factors of production (labour, capital and land) and most importantly conformity to development priorities of the state, then naturally the issue of land grabbing and possible consequences can be effectively tackled.

Currently, too much emphasis is placed on the fiscal incentives as an instrument to promote SEZ. In fact, there exists a uniform incentive structure with regards to all the sectors. Instead, the government can also think of restructuring the incentives based on the development priorities of each sectors, that is, devising different incentive slabs applicable to different sectors, with an emphasis on the comparative advantage of each region. Furthermore, given the turf between the Ministry of Commerce and Industry and Ministry of Finance, and also due to cumbersome procedures involved in claiming incentives in real terms, SEZ investors find it very difficult to claim many such incentives. Moreover, incentives are necessary but not a sufficient condition for export promotion. Furthermore, in the absence of effective institutional arrangements and infrastructure facilities, it may be very difficult to sustain investors' confidence in the promotion of SEZs. For instance, the SEZ policy, in the present context, appears to be a policy devised by the central government and followed by the state governments; however, it has consistently failed to consider the problems and prospects at the zonal level. All the seven conventional SEZs of the country are confronted with specific problems and prospects, which need policy attention.[3] The fact is that these issues do not get reflected either in the central or state government SEZ policy. To remedy this, it is necessary to persuade each state government to periodically survey the scenario in zones within its jurisdiction and to deal with the issues accordingly. Furthermore, there are sector-specific requirements and problems involved in the promotion of SEZs. Thus, instead of having a uniform policy applicable to all states/zones and sectors, it is desirable to revisit the policy based on the sector and zone-specific problems and prospects. This could provide a more realistic and investor friendly atmosphere for achieving the stated objectives underlying of SEZs in the country. It is also important to ensure that no undue emphasis is placed on incentives for SEZs, as it can cause a drain on the government exchequer (at least in the short term).

As per the current SEZ policy, the supervision of all the upcoming SEZs is assigned to one of the seven conventional SEZ development

---

3   This is explained in detail in chapter 5.

commissioners. Although there is one assistant development commissioner officer to look after the day-to-day activities, he does not have all the required administrative powers to deal with different issues. Thus, other than day-to-day administrative matters, all major issues have to be referred to respective development commissioners. The government on its part may argue that such a policy is necessary to reduce the revenue expenditure involved in the administrative maintenance in each zone. But such economy measures may retard the speed at which these offices could operate in terms of the pressure it could create with the available staff put under the development commissioner officer. Therefore, it is necessary to think of alternative approaches in this respect.

Due care should be exercised while allocating land to SEZs for manufacturing activities. The experience of Shenzhen SEZ is a classic example in this respect as it had resulted in conversion of agricultural land to manufacturing and related activities. As a result, over the last three decades there has been a substantial decline in the land available for agricultural activities in China. Currently, Shenzhen is highly dependent on other provinces for its food supply, thereby, fuelling further the problem of inflation in the region. However, unlike China, SEZ in India are not limited to any region/state. In fact, within a few years since their introduction, SEZs have spread all over the country. Moreover, the process of implementation of SEZ policy in India has been different from that of China. In India, so far, farmers have no stake in the emerging SEZs. Further, there is no assurance forthcoming from the government with regard to providing employment for the locals in the respective zones nor has there been any effort on the government's part to train the displaced farmers to be employable in industrial activities. SEZ Act, 2005 takes away labour related powers from the jurisdiction of the state labour commissioners and vests it in development commissioners of the respective zones. The apparent objective behind this move is to promote hassles-free business environment, specifically to forestall avoidable labour unrest and the consequent loss of production and profits. However, it is observed that contrary to SEZ provisions, different practices are followed across zones. Furthermore, the SEZ policy is not very clear about the sources from which the needed labour force can be drawn. It is assumed that the labour market in each zone supplies the required labour force with the result that there is a limited scope for government intervention. This, however, in the long run, might give scope for middlemen to exploit workers. Thus, there is a pressing need for the government intervention in this area. Government supervision can not only assure the supply of required manpower to these zones but also prevent the exploitation of labour, by middlemen/agents. As a first step in this direction, the government can focus on promoting educational institutions in the regions according to the requirements of each zone.

Bibliography

Abid Hussian Committee. 1984. *Report of the Committee on Trade Policies*. New Delhi: Ministry of Commerce, Government of India.

Aggarwal, Aradhana. 2004. 'Export Processing Zones in India: Analysis of the Export Performance'. ICRIER Working Paper No. 148, Indian Council of Research in International Economic Relations (ICRIER), New Delhi.

———. 2005. 'Performance of Export Processing Zones: A Comparative Analysis of India, Sri Lanka, and Bangladesh'. ICRIER Working Paper No. 155, Indian Council of Research in International Economic Relations ICRIER, New Delhi.

———. 2006. 'Special Economic Zones: Revisiting the Policy Debate'. *Economic and Political Weekly* 41(43–44): 4533–36.

———. May 2007. '"SEZs in India": A Quantitative Assessment of Costs and Benefits'. Seminar paper presented in ICRIER Workshop on SEZs and its Impacts on Export Promotion in India, New Delhi.

———. 2010. 'Economic Impacts of SEZs: Theoretical Approaches and analysis of Newly Notified SEZs in India'. MPRA Paper 20902, 1–59.

———. 2012. *Socio Economic Impact of Special Economic Zones in India*. India: Oxford University Press.

Ahulwalia, Isher Judge. 2009. 'Trade Liberalisation and Industrial Performance – a disaggregated view of Indian manufacturing in the 1990s'. In *Readings in Indian Agriculture and Industry*, edited by K. L. Krishna and Uma Kapila, 431–64. New Delhi: Academic Foundations.

Amirahamdi, Hooshang, and Weiping Wu.1995. 'Export Processing Zones in Asia'. *Asian Survey* 35: 828–49.

Armas, Enrique Blanco de and Sadni-Lallab Mustapha. 2002. 'A Review of the Role and Impact of EPZs in the World Trade: The Case of Mexico'. Working Papers, W.P. 02-07 Documents, De Travail, France.

Arora, O. P. 2003. Compilation of Circulars on EPZ/SEZ/EOU issued by CBEC, DGFT and RBI. New Delhi: M/s Anmkur Arora Associates.

Bahl, S. K. 1996. 'China's Economic and Technological Development Zones'. In *China's Economic Reforms: The Role of Special Economic Zones and Economic and Technological Development Zones*, edited by S. P. Gupta, 75–128. New Delhi: Allied Publishers Limited.

Banerjee, Abhijit Vinayak, Pranab Bardhan, Kaushik Basu, Mrinall Datta Chaudhary, Mathesh Ghattak, Ashok Sanjay Guha, Mukul Majumdar, Dilip Mookherjee, and Deebray Ray. 2007. 'Beyond Nandigram: Industrialization in West Bengal'. *Economic and Political Weekly* 42 (17): 1487–89.

Barro, R. J. and X. Sala-i-Martin. 1991. 'Convergence across States and Regions'. *Brookings Papers on Economic Activity* 1: 107–58.

Battese, G. E. and T. Coelli. 1995. 'A Model for Technical Efficiency Effects in a Stochastic Production Function for Panel Data'. *Empirical Economics* 20: 325–32.

Bhaduri, Amit. 2007. 'Alternatives in Industrialization'. *Economic and Political Weekly* 42 (18):1597–601.

Bose, D. K. 2007. 'Land Acquisition in West Bengal'. *Economic and Political Weekly* 42 (17). 1574–82.

Bussolo, Maurizio, and Nicita Alessandro. 2005. 'Trade Policy Reforms'. In *Analysing the Distributional Impacts of Reforms A Practitioners Guide to Trade, Monetary, and Exchange Rate Policy, Utility Provision, Agricultural Markets, Land Policy and Education*, edited by Coudoel Aline and Stefano Paternostro, 1–38. Washington, D.C.: World Bank.

Cai, Y. 2003. 'Collective Ownership or Cadres Ownership? The Non Agricultural Use of Farmland in China'. *The China Quarterly* 175: 662–80.

Cannan, Edwin. 1892. 'The Origin of the Law of Diminishing Returns 1813-15'. *Economic Journal* 2 (5): 53–69.

Cartier, Carolyn. 2001. 'Zone Fever, the Arable Land Debate and Real Estate Speculation: China's Evolving Land Use Regime and its Geographical Contradictions'. *Journal of Contemporary China* 10 (28): 445–69.

Chen, Jie. 2007. 'Rapid Urbanization in China: A Real Challenge to Soil Protection and Food Security'. *Catena* 69 (1): 1–15.

Chen, J. 1998. 'Social Costs Benefits Analysis of China's Shenzhen Special Economic Zones'. *Development Policy Review* 11 (3): 261–72.

Chen, Xiangmang. 1987. 'Magic and Myth of Migration: A Case Study of SEZs in China'. *Asia-Pacific Population Journal* 2 (3): 57–76.

Chu, David K. Y. 1985. 'Population Growth and Related Issues'. In *Modernization in China: The Case of Shenzhen Special Economic Zone*, edited by K. Y. Wong and David K. Y. Chu, 131–39. Hong Kong: Oxford University Press.

Cling, J. P. and G. Letilly. 2001. *Export Processing Zones, A Threatened Instrument for Global Economy Insertion?* Paris: DT/2001/17, Development Institutions and Analyses de Long terne International (DIAL).

Cook, I., Ramachandra Bhatta and Vidya Dinker. 2013. 'The Multiple Displacements of Mangalore Special Economic Zone'. *Economic and Political Weekly* 48 (33): 40–46.

Dagli Committee. 1979. *Report of the Committee on Controls and Subsidies*. New Delhi: Ministry of Commerce, Government of India.

Deepika, M. G. and R. S. Deshpande. 2003. 'Trade Policy and Determinants of Trade in Agriculture'. Working Paper No. 118, Institute for Social and Economic Change, Bangalore.

Ebrill, Liam, Janet Stotsky and Reint Gropp. 1999. 'Revenue Implications of Trade Liberalization'. International Monetary Fund Occasional Paper No. 180, Washington.

Engman, Michael, Osamu Onodera and Enrico Pinali. 2007. 'Export Processing Zones Past and Future Role in Trade and Development'. OECD Trade Policy Working Papers No. 53, OECD Publishing, France.

Fujita, Masahisa, and Dapeng Hu. 2001. 'Regional Disparity in China 1985–1994: The Effects of Globalization and Economic Liberalization'. *The Annals of Regional Science* 35: 3–37.

Ge, Wei. 1999. 'Special Economic Zone and Opening of the Chinese Economy: Some Lesson for Economic Liberalization'. *World Development* 27 (7): 1267–85.

Gill, Sucha Singh. 2007. 'Special Economic Zones and Displacement–Need for an Alternative Model'. *Man and Development*, 24 (4): 95–106.

Goldar, Bishwanath. 2002. 'Trade Liberalization and Manufacturing Employment: The Case of India'. Employment Paper 2002/34, International Labour Organization, Geneva.

Gopalakrishnan, Shankar. 2007. 'Negative Aspects of Special Economic Zones in China'. *Economic and Political Weekly* 42 (17): 1492–94.

Goswami, Bhaskar. 2007. 'Special Economic Zones Lessons from China, in Motion Magazine'. *NPC Production*, New York. Accessed 30 August 2007, available at: http://www.inmotionmagazine.com/opin/bg_sez_china.html.

Government of Andhra Pradesh. 2002a. 'Andhra Pradesh Government Notification F.O. Rt. No. 1515'. *100% Units Located in Export Processing Zones/Special economic Zones in the State Declare as Public Utility Service.* Hyderabad: Labour Employment Training and Factories (Lab–I) Department Government of Andhra Pradesh.

———. 2002b. 'Andhra Pradesh Government Notification No. 277'. *Exemption from Levy of Tax on the Entertainment held within Special Economic Zones.* Hyderabad: Government of Andhra Pradesh.

———. 2002c. 'Andhra Pradesh Government Notification No. 290'. *5% Exemption from Payment of Stamp Duty and Registration Fee on Transfer of Lands meant for Industrial use in the Special Economic Zones Area Amendment.* Hyderabad: Government of Andhra Pradesh.

———. 2002d. 'Andhra Pradesh Government Notification No. G.O. Ms. No. 356, Revenue (CT-III)'. *Exemption from Levy Tax on the Entertainment held within Special Economic Zones.* Hyderabad: Revenue Department. Government of Andhra Pradesh.

———. 2002e. 'Andhra Pradesh Government Notification No. G.O. Ms. No. 333, Revenue (CT-III)'. *Exemption from Levy of Sales Tax on Autoclaved Aerated Concrete (ACC) Blocks.* Hyderabad: Revenue Department, Government of Andhra Pradesh.

———. 2002f. 'Andhra Pradesh Government Notification No. G.O. Ms. No. 355, Revenue (CT-III)'. *Exemption from Levy of Tax on the Luxuries provided within Special Economic Zones.* Hyderabad: Revenue Department, Government of Andhra Pradesh.

———. 2002g. 'Andhra Pradesh Government Notification No. G.O.Ms 159'. *Infrastructure Andhra Pradesh Special Economic Zones (APSEZ) Policy Framework at APSEZ adapted to Vishakhapatnam Export Processing Zones (VSEZ).* Hyderabad: Industries and Commerce (INF) Department, Government of Andhra Pradesh.

———. 2002h. 'Andhra Pradesh Government Notification No. G.O.Ms 72'. *Establishment of Special Economic Zones (SEZ) in Andhra Pradesh-Policy Framework on Environment and Forests and APPOB.* Hyderabad: Environment, Forests, Sciences and Technology (ENV) Department, Government of Andhra Pradesh.

———. 2002i. 'Andhra Pradesh Government Notification No. G.O.Ms. No. 306-Special Economic Zones'. *Exemption from Levy of Sale Tax on the Inputs Supplied by Units'.* Hyderabad: Government of Andhra Pradesh.

———. 2002j. 'Andhra Pradesh Government Notification No G.O.R t. No. 1544'. *Declaration of Power of the Commissioner of Labour to the Development Commissioner of Export Promotion Zones and Special Economic Zones in AP.* Hyderabad: Labour Employment and Training and Factories (Lab IV) Department, Government of Andhra Pradesh.

———. 2002k. 'Andhra Pradesh Government Notification No. G.O.Rt.No.1544'. *Labour Employment Training Factoriesm.* Hyderabad: (LAB-IV) Department, Government of Andhra Pradesh.

———. 2002l. 'Andhra Pradesh Government Notification No. G.O.Rt.No.1545'. *Labour Employment Training Factories.* Hyderabad: (LAB-IV) Department, Government of Andhra Pradesh.

Government of Chandigarh. 2005. 'Chandigarh Government Notification No. 227/IT//2005/2122' on *SEZS policy of Chandigarh Administration.* Chandigarh: Information Technology Department, Government of Chandigarh.

Government of Gujarat. 2004. *Gujarat SEZs Act No. 11 of 2004.* Ahmedabad: Ahmedabad Legislative and Parliamentary Affairs Department, Government of Gujarat.

Government of Haryana. 2005. *The Haryana Special Economic Zone Act 2005.* Chandigarh: Haryana Act No. 9 of 2006, Government of Haryana.

Government of India (Various Issues during 1964–65 to 2009–10). *Economic Survey of India.* New Delhi: Ministry of Finance, Government of India.

———. 1990. *EXIM Policy Statement 1990.* New Delhi: Ministry of Commerce, Government of India.

———. 1997. *EXIM Policy Statement 1997-2002.* New Delhi: Ministry of Commerce, Government of India.

———. 2000. *EXIM Policy Statement 2000-01.* New Delhi: Ministry of Commerce, Government of India.

———. 2001a. *EXIM Policy Statement 2001-02.* New Delhi: Ministry of Commerce, Government of India.

———. 2001b. *EXIM Policy Statement 2000-01.* New Delhi: Ministry of Commerce.

———. 2002. *EXIM Policy Statement 2002-07.* New Delhi: Ministry of Commerce, Government of India.

———. 2005. *The Special Economic Zones Act 2005, No. 28.* New Delhi: Ministry of Law and Justice, Government of India.

———. 2006. *The Special Economic Zones. Rules 2006.* New Delhi: Ministry of Commerce and Industry (Department of Commerce), Government of India.

———. 2009. *RBI Circular allowing SEZ Developer to maintain EEFC Account.* RBI/2009-10/275 A.P., (DIR Series) Circular No. 22. New Delhi: Ministry of Finance, Government of India.

———. 2010a. *Exemption to ATMs in SEZ from being treated as OBUs.* New Delhi: Ministry of Commerce and Industry, Government of India.

———. 2010b. *Exemption to SEZ Developers from obtaining Distribution License.* New Delhi: Government of India, Ministry of Commerce and Industry.

———. 2010c. *Hazardous Wastes Management, Handling and Transboundary Movement Third Amendment Rules.* 2010. New Delhi: Ministry of Environment and Forests, Government of India.

———. 2010d. *Notification Authorizing DCs of SEZs to be the Enforcement Officer for the Purpose of Section 21 of SEZ Act, 2005.* New Delhi: Ministry of Commerce and Industry, Government of India.

———. 2010e. *Notification for Operationalizing Sections 20, 21 and 22 of SEZ Act, 2005.* New Delhi: Ministry of Commerce and Industry, Government of India.

———. 2010f. *Union Budget 2010-2011. New Delhi:* Ministry of Finance, Government of India.

————. 2011. *Economic Survey of India*. New Delhi: Ministry of Finance, Government of India.

————. 2012. *Economic Survey of India*. New Delhi: Ministry of Finance, Government of India.

Government of Jharkhand. 2003. *Jharkhand Government Notification No. 2460 on SEZ*. Ranchi: Department of Industries, Government of Jharkhand.

Government of Karnataka. 2002a. *Karnataka Government Notification (I) No. 79/2000-cus and No. 41/2000-CE*. Bangalore: Department of Energy, Government of Karnataka.

————. 2002b. *Karnataka Government Notification No. S. O. 60 (E)*. Bangalore: Forest, Ecology and Environment Department, Government of Karnataka.

————. 2003a. *Karnataka Government Notification No. DE. 201 PTC 2001, Setting Up of Power Plants in SEZs*. Bangalore: Department of Energy, Government of Karnataka.

————. 2003b. *Karnataka Government Notification (II) No. DD116 KABSANI 2002 (Part I)*. Bangalore: Labour Department, Government of Karnataka.

————. 2003c. *Karnataka Government Notification No. DD116 KABSANI 2002 (Part I)*. Bangalore: Labour Department, Government of Karnataka.

————. 2003d. *Karnataka Government Notification No. DD 116 KABANI 2002–'Issues Relating to Labour Concerning SEZ'*. Bangalore: Department of Energy, Government of Karnataka.

————. 2003e. *Karnataka Government Notification No. FD 96 CSL 2003 (1)–'Sales Tax Exemption to SEZs Units'*. Bangalore: Karnataka Government Secretariat, Vidhana Soudha, Government of Karnataka.

————. 2003f. *Karnataka Government Notification No. FD 96 CSL 2003 (4)*. Bangalore: Finance Department, Government of Karnataka.

————. 2003g. *Karnataka Government Notification No. FD 96 CSL 2003 (2)–'Sales Tax Exemption to SEZs Developers and Setting up of Units'*. Bangalore: Karnataka Government Secretariat, Vidhana Soudha.

————. 2003h. *Karnataka Government Notification No. FD 96 CSL 2003 (3)–'Exemption from Entry Tax for SEZs units and Developers'*. Bangalore: Karnataka Government Secretariat, Vidhana Soudha.

————. 2003i. *Karnataka Government Notification No. FD 96 CSL 2003 (4)–'Reduction in Tax on Supply of Petroleum Products to SEZs'*. Bangalore: Karnataka Government Secretariat, Vidhana Soudha.

————. 2003j. *Karnataka Government Notification No. FD 96 CSL 2003(3)*. Bangalore: Department of Finance, Government of Karnataka.

————. 2003j. *Karnataka Government Notification No. FEE 32 ENV*

2001–'Environment Clearance to SEZs'. Bangalore: Karnataka Government Forest, Ecology and Environment Department, Government of Karnataka.

———. 2003k. The Karnataka Special Economic Zones Development Bill, 2003 (L.A Bill No 24 of 2003). Bangalore: Government of Karnataka.

———. 2009a. *Karnataka Government Notification No DD (ID)/SEZ/MRC/95/2009-10 on Operational Guidelines for administration of state Policy on SEZs-2009.* Bangalore: Directorate of Industries and Commerce, Government of Karnataka.

———. 2009b. *State Policy for SEZs 2009.* Bangalore: Government of Karnataka.

Government of Kerala. 2008. *Kerala Government Policies on Special Economic Zones: 2008.* Trivandrum: Government of Kerala.

Government of Madhya Pradesh. 2003. *The Indore Special Economic Zone'.* (Special Provisions) Act, 2003. Indore: Government of Madhya Pradesh.

Government of Maharashtra. 2001a. *Maharashtra Government Policy on SEZs, Government of Maharashtra, SEZs Resolution No. 2001/(152)/IND-2.* Mumbai: Industries, Energy and Labour Department, Government of Maharashtra.

———. 2001b. *Maharashtra Government Policy on SEZ Resolution No. SEZ 2001/ (152) IND-2.* Mumbai: Industries, Energy and Labour Department, Government of Maharashtra.

Government of Orissa. 2003. *Orissa Government Policies on Special Economic Zone.* Bhubaneswar: Industrial Department Government of Orissa.

Government of Punjab. 2009. *Punjab Government Notification Act No. 17 of 2009.* Chandigarh: Department of Legal and Legislative Affairs, Government of Punjab.

———. 2005. *Punjab Government Notification No. /58/2002/2HB/4630 o Punjab Special Economic Zone Policy 2005.* Chandigarh: Ministry of Industries and Commerce, Government of Punjab.

Government of Rajasthan. 2003. *Rajasthan Government's SEZs Act Notification No. F.4(6)Gidhi/2/2003.* Jaipur: Law Department, Government of Rajasthan.

Government of Tamil Nadu. 2005a. *Tamil Nadu Acquisition of Land for Industrial Purpose (Amendment) Act No 17 of 2005.* Chennai: Government of Tamil Nadu.

———. 2005b. *Tamil Nadu Special Economic Zones Act No 18 of 2005.* Chennai: Government of Tamil Nadu.

Government of Uttar Pradesh. 2002. *Uttar Pradesh Government Policy on SEZ.* Lucknow: Laghu Udyog Avam Niryat Protsahan Anubhag-4, Government of Uttar Pradesh.

Government of West Bengal. 2003. *The West Bengal Special Economic Zones.* Kolkata: Government of West Bengal, Kolkata.

Grasset, Jeremy, and Frederic Landy. 2007. 'Special Economic Zones in India–Between International Integration and Real Estate Speculation'. *Man and Development* 29 (4): 63–74.

Greenway, David, and Chris Milner. 1991. 'Fiscal Dependence on Trade Taxes and Trade Policy Reform'. *Journal of Development Studie* 27 (3): 95–132.

Gupta, K. R. 2008. *Special Economic Zones: Issues, Laws and Procedures* (Vol. 1 and 2). New Delhi: Atlantic Publication and Distribution.

Hameed, Shahul P. M. 1996. 'China's Special Economic Zones'. In *China's Economic Reforms: The Role of Special Economic Zones and Economic and Technological Development Zones*, edited by S. P. Gupta, 35–74. New Delhi: Allied Publishers Limited.

Hill, Hal, and K. P. Kalirajan. 1993. 'Small Enterprises and Firm Level Technical Efficiency in the Indonesian Garment Industry'. *Applied Economics* 25 (9): 1137–44.

Ho, Samuel P. S. and George C. S. Lin 2004. 'Converting Land to non-Agricultural Uses in China's Coastal Provinces'. *Modern China* 30 (1): 81–112.

Huang, Yiping. 1998. *Agricultural Reform in China: Getting Institutional Framework*. Cambridge: Cambridge University Press.

Hull, Terrence. 1990. 'Recent Trends in Sex Ratio at Birth in China'. *Population and Development Review* 16 (1): 63–83.

IIFT. 1990. 'Exports Processing Zones in India: A Case study of Kandla Free Trade Zone'. Indian Institute of Foreign Trade Occasional Paper, New Delhi.

ILO. 2006. 'Database on Export Processing Zones (Revisited)'. ILO Working Paper 251, Geneva. Accessed December 2008, available at: http://www.ilo.org/public/libdoc/ilo/2007/107B09_80_engl.pdf.

ITC. 2000. 'The Trade Performance Index'. Document Prepared by International Trade Center (ITC)-Market Analysis Section.

Iyengar, N. S. and P. Sudharshan. 1982. 'A Method of Classifying Regions from Multivariate Data'. *Economic and Political Weekly* 17 (51): 2047–52.

Jayanthakumaran, Kankesu. 2002. 'An Overview of Export Processing Zones: Selected Asian Countries'. Working Paper Series 2002, University of Wollongong.

————. 2003. 'Benefit-Cost Appraisals of Export Processing Zones: A Survey of the Literature'. *Development Policy Review* 21(1): 51–65.

Jenkins, Mauricio, Gerardo Esquivel and Felipe Larraín B. August 1998. 'Export Processing Zones in Central America'. Development Discussion Paper, No. 4, Harvard Institute for International Development, Harvard, Central America.

Jones, Derek C, Cheng Li and Ann L. Owen, 2003. 'Growth and Regional Inequality in China during the Reform Era'. *China Economic Review* 14 (2): 186–200.

Kasturi, Kannan. 2008. 'Of Public Purpose and Private Profit'. *Seminar* 582.

Kingston, J. L. 1973. 'Exports Instability in Latin America: The Postwar Statistical Record'. *Journal of Developing Areas* 7 (3): 381–96.

————. 1976. 'Exports Concentration and Exports Performance in Developing Countries: 1954–67'. *Journal of Development Studies* 12 (4): 311–19.

Koslowski, Rey. 1992. 'Market Institutions, East European Reform, and Economic Theory'. *Journal of Economic Theory* 26 (3): 673–705.

Kumar, Rajiv. 1987. 'Performance of Foreign and Domestic Firms in Export Processing Zones'. *World Development* 15 (10/11): 130–19.

————. 1989. *Indian Export Processing Zones: An Evaluation.* New Delhi: Oxford University Press.

Kundra, Ashok. 2000. *The Performance of India's Export Zones – A Comparison with Chinese Approach.* New Delhi: Sage Publication.

Kusago, T. and Zafiris Tzannatos. 1998. 'Export Processing Zones: A Review in Need of Update'. *Social Protection Group, Human Development Network. The World Bank, SP Discussion Paper 9802.* Washington, D.C.: The World Bank.

Lardy, Nicholas R. 1993. 'Recasting of Economic Systems Structural Reforms in Agriculture and Industry'. In *China in the Era of Deng Xioping, An East Gate Book*, edited by Michael Ying Maukau and Susan H. Marsh. New York Press: An east Gate Book.

————. 1994. *China in the World Economy.* Washington, DC: Institute for International Economics.

————. 2007. 'Trade Liberalization and its Role in Chinese Economic Growth'. In *India's and China's Recent Experience with Reform and Growth*, edited by Tseng Wando and David Cowen, 158–69. IMF, Great Britain: Palgrave Macmillan.

Laxmanan, L. 2009. *'Evolution of Special Economic Zones and Some Issues: The Indian Experiences'.* The RBI Staff Studies, Department of Economic Analysis and Policy.

Levien, Michael. 2011. 'Rationalising Dispossession: The Land Acquisition and Resettlement Bills'. *Economic and Political Weekly* 46 (11): 66–71.

Li, Shaomin. 2004. 'The Puzzle of Firm Performance in China: An Institutional Explanation'. *Economics of Planning* 37: 47–68.

Lichtenberg, Erik, and Chengri Ding. 2008. 'Assessing Farmland Protection Policy in China'. *Land Use Policy* 25 (1): 59–68.

Madani, Dorasti. 1999. 'A Review of the Role and Impact of Export Processing Zone'. Policy Research Working Paper No. 2238, Development Research Group Trade, The World Bank.

Maddala, G. S. 1979. 'A Note on the Form of the Production Function and Productivity'. In *Measurement and Interpretation of Productivity*, 309–17. Washington, D.C.: National Research Council.

Majumudar, Manab. 2007. 'Approaching Special Economic Zones–The Debate'. *Man and Development* 29 (4): 1–24.

Masell, Benton, F. 1970. 'Exports Instability and Economic Growth'. *American Economic Review* 60: 618–30.

Matlanyane, Adelaide, and Chris Harmse. 2002. 'Revenue Implications of Trade Liberalization in South Africa'. *South African Journal of Economics* 70 (2): 155–61.

Menon, Narayan S. and Soumya Kanti Mitra. 2009. 'Special Economic Zones: The Rationale'. CPR Occasional Paper Series 1, 33–38. New Delhi.

Mitra, Siddhartha. 2007. 'Special Economic Zones – Rationale and Pitfalls in Implementations'. *Man and Development* 24 (4): 39–48.

Mukherjee, Kankana and Subhash C. Ray. 2004. 'Technical Efficiency and its Dynamics in Indian Manufacturing: An Inter State Analysis'. Working Paper Series 2004, No. 18, Department of Economics, University of Connecticut, Stamford.

————. 2005. 'Technical Efficiency and its Dynamics in Indian Manufacturing: An Inter State Analysis'. *Indian Economic Review* 40 (2): 101–26.

Mukhopadhyay, Partha. 2009. 'The Promised Land of SEZs', CPR Occasional Paper Series 2, 39–60, New Delhi.

Mukhopadhay, Partha, and Kanhu Charan Pradhan. 2009. 'Location of SEZs and Policy Benefits What Does the Data Say?' CPR Discussion Paper Series 3, 61–84, New Delhi.

Mukhopadhyay, Sukumar. May 2007. 'Costs and Benefits of Tax Exemption for Export Promotion Scheme'. Seminar paper presented in ICRIER Workshop on SEZs and Its Impacts on Export Promotion in India, New Delhi.

Narayanan, Raviprasad. 2006. 'The Politics of Reforms in China: Deng, Jiang and Hu'. *Strategic Analysis* 30 (2): 329–53.

National Statistics Bureau. 2011. *Chinese Statistical Year Book (CSY)*. Beijing: China Statistical Press.

Nayyar, Deepak. 1976. 'India's Export Performance in the 1970s'. *Economic and Political Weekly* 11 (5): 731–43.

Ng, Yen-Tak, and David K. Y. Chu. 1985. 'The Geographical Endowment of China's Special Economic Zones'. In *Modernization in China: The Case of Special Economic Zone*, edited by K. Y. Wong and David K. Y. Chu, 40–56. Hong Kong: Oxford University Press.

Nishitateno, Sonoko. 1983. 'China's Special Economic Zones: Experimental Units for Economic Reform'. *The International and Comparative Law Quarterly* 32 (1): 175–85.

Nurkse, R. 1953. *Problems of Capital Formation in Underdeveloped Countries*. Oxford: Basil Blackwell.

Oborne, Michael West. 1986. *China's Special Economic Zones*. Paris: Development Centre of the Organization for Economic Co-operation and Development, OECD.

Ota, Tatsuyuki. 2003. 'The Role of SEZs in Chinese Economic Development as Compared with Asian Export Processing Zones: 1979-85'. *Asia in Extenso March*. Accessed October 2007, available at: http://www.iae.univ-poitiers.fr/EURO-ASIE/Docs/Asia-in-Extenso-Ota-mars2003.pdf.

Palit, Amitensu, and Subhomoy Bhattacharjee. 2008. *Special Economic Zones in India Myths and Realities*. New Delhi: Anthem Press.

Park, J. 1997. *The Special Economic Zones of China and their Impact on the Economic Development of China*. Westport, London: PRAEGER.

Patnaik, Prabhat. 2007. 'In the Aftermath of Nandigram'. *Economic and Political Weekly* 46 (21): 1893–94.

Peimin, L. 2007. 'A Case Study on the Settlement of Rural Women Affected by Land Requisitioning in China'. *Journal of Contemporary China* 16 (50): 133–48.

People Republic of China. 1980. *Regulations of the People's Republic of China on Special Economic Zone*. Beijing.

Prebisch, R. 1959. 'Commercial Policy in the Underdeveloped Countries'. *American Economic Review* 49 (2) (Papers and Proceedings of seventy first annual meeting of the American Economic Associations): 251–73.

Ramachandran, V. and R. Cleetus. 1999. *Export Processing Zones: The Chinese Experience and its Lessons for Tamil Nadu*. World Bank, Washington, DC. Mimeo.

Rao, R. Kavitha. 8 September 2007. 'Special Economic Zone-Brain or Drain'. *Business Standard*, New Delhi.

Reserve Bank of India. 2007. *'Annual Report on Currency and Finance 2007-08'*. Mumbai: RBI.

Review Committee on Electronics. 1979. *Report of the committee on Electronics*. New-Delhi: Ministry of Commerce, Government of India.

Sampat, Preeti. 2008. 'Special Economic Zones in India'. *Economic and Political Weekly* 43 (28): 25–30.

Sarma E. R. S. 2007. 'Help the Rich, Hurt the Poor: Case of Special Economic Zones'. *Economic and Political Weekly* 42 (21): 1900–02.

Sen, Amartya and Jean Drèze. 1999. *India and China, in Poverty and Famines, Hunger and Public Action, India Economic Development and Social Opportunity*, 57–86. New Delhi: Oxford University Press.

Shah, Deepak. 2009. 'Special Economic Zones in India: A Review of Investment, Trade, Employment Generation and Impact Assessment'. *Indian Journal of Agricultural Economics* 64 (3): 431–41.

Sharma E. R. S. 2007. 'Help the Rich, Hurt the Poor: Case of Special Economic Zones'. *Economic and Political Weekly* XLII (8): 1900–02.

Shenzhen Statistics Bureau. 2013. *Shenzhen Statistical Year Book (SZSY)*. China: China Statistical Press.

Sivaramakrishnan, K. C. 2009. 'Special Economic Zones: Issues of Urban Growth and Management'. CPR Occasional Paper Series 4, New Delhi.

Soni, Nikunj, Belinda Harries and Betty Zineer-Toa. 2007. 'Responding to the Revenue Consequences of Trade Reforms in the Forum Island Countries'. Final Report, Port Vila.

Srinivasan, T. 2002. 'China and India: Economic Performance, Competition and Cooperation'. Paper Presented at a Seminar on WTO Accession, Policy Reforms and Poverty Organized by the World Trade Organization, Beijing.

Stiglitz, Joseph E. and Andrew, Chartlon. 2005. *Fair Trade for All, How Trade Can Promote Development*. New York: Oxford University Press.

Sundarapandian, M. 2012. *Development of Special Economic Zones in India: Policies and Issues* (Vol 1 and 2). New Delhi: Concept Publishing Company Pvt Ltd.

Tandon Committee.1980. *Report of the committee on Export Strategy*. New Delhi: Ministry of Commerce, Government of India.

Tatsuyuki, Ota. March 2003. 'The Role of SEZs in Chinese Economic Development as Compared with Asian Export Processing Zones: 1979–85'. *Asia in Extenso*.

Vijayabhaskar, M. 2010. 'Saving Agricultural Labour from Agriculture: SEZs and Politics of Silence in Tamil Nadu'. *Economic and Political Weekly* 45 (06): 36–43.

Wall, David. 1993. 'China's Economic Reform and Opening-Up Process: The Role of the Special Economic Zones'. *Development Policy Review* 11(3): 243–60.

Warr, P. G. 1988. 'Export Processing Zones – The Economies of Enclave Manufacturing'. *World Bank Research Observer* 4 (1): 65–88.

Working Paper 88/5, The Australian National University, Australia.

———. (1989). 'Export Processing Zones – The Economies of Enclave Manufacturing'. *World Bank Research Observer* 4 (1): 65–87.

www.lib.utexas.edu/maps/china.html

www.sezindia.nic.in

Wong, K. Y. and David K. Y. Chu. 1985a. *Modernization in China: The Case of Special Economic Zone*. Hong Kong: Oxford University Press.

———. 1985b. 'Export Processing Zones and Special Economic Zones as Locomotives of Export-led Economic Growth'. In *Modernization in China: The Case of Shenzhen Special Economic Zone*, edited by K. Y. Wong and David K. Y. Chu, 89–107. Hong Kong: Oxford University Press.

Wong, Edy L. 1987. 'Recent Development in China's Special Economic Zone: Problems and Prognosis'. *The Developing Economies* 25 (1): 73–86.

World Bank. 1983. *China: Socialist Economic Development.* Washington, D.C.: World Bank.

————. 1992. 'Export Processing Zone'. Policy and Research Series Paper 20, Industry and Energy Department, Washington, D.C.

Wu, Weiping. 1999. *Pioneering Economic Reforms in China's Special Economic Zones: the Promotion of Foreign Investment and Technology Transfers in Shenzhen.* London: Ashgate Publishing Limited.

Yang, Hong and Xiubin Li. 2000. 'Cultivated Land and Food Supply in China'. *Land Use Policy* 17 (2): 73–88.

Yeh, Anthony G.O. 1985. 'Physical Planning'. In *Modernization in China: The Case of Shenzhen Special Economic Zone,* edited by K. Y. Wong and David K. Y. Chu, 108–30. Hong Kong: Oxford University Press.

Yeung, Yue-man, Joana Lee and Gordon Kee. 2009. 'China's Special Economic Zones at 30'. *Eurasian Geography* 50 (2): 222–40.

Zafar, Ali. 2005. 'Revenue and Fiscal Impact of Trade Liberalization: The Case of Niger'. World Bank Policy Research Working Paper 3500, World Bank, Washington, D.C.

Zeng, Douglous Zhina. 2011. 'How do Special Economic Zones and Industrial Clusters Drive China's Rapid Development'. World Bank Policy Research Working Paper 5583, The World Bank, Washington, D.C.

Zheng, Tianxiang, Qingaquan Wei and David K. Y. Chu. 1985. 'Agriculture Land Use Patterns and Export Potential'. In *Modernization in China: The Case of Shenzhen Special Economic Zone,* edited by K. Y. Wong and David K. Y. Chu. Hong Kong: Oxford University Press.

Index